THE LIBRARY OF HOLOCAUST TESTIMONIES

My Hometown Concentration Camp

The Library of Holocaust Testimonies

Editors: Antony Polonsky, Sir Martin Gilbert CBE, Aubrey Newman,
Raphael F. Scharf, Ben Helfgott MBE

Under the auspices of the Yad Vashem Committee of the Board of
Deputies of British Jews and the Centre for Holocaust Studies,
University of Leicester

My Hometown Concentration Camp

A Survivor's Account of Life in the Kraków Ghetto and Płaszów Concentration Camp

BERNARD OFFEN
with Norman G. Jacobs

Witness and survivor of the Kraków Ghetto, Płaszów, Julag, Mauthausen, Auschwitz-Birkenau, and Dachau-Kaufering Concentration Camps

VALLENTINE MITCHELL
LONDON • PORTLAND, OR

First published in 2008 by
VALLENTINE MITCHELL

920 NE 58th Avenue, Suite 300
Portland, Oregon 97213-3786

Suite 314, Premier House
Edgware, Middlesex HA8 7BJ

www.vmbooks.com
www.bernardoffen.org

British Library Cataloguing in Publication Data

Offen, Bernard
 My hometown concentration camp : a survivor's account of
 life in the Krakow ghetto and Plaszow Concentration Camp. –
 (The library of Holocaust testimonies)
 1. Offen, Bernard 2. Plaszow (Concentration camp)
 3. Holocaust, Jewish (1939–1945) – Poland – Personal
 narratives 4. Jews – Persecutions – Poland – History – 20th
 century
 I. Title II. Jacobs, Norman A.
 940.5'318'092

ISBN 978 0 85303 636 4
ISSN 1363 3759

Library of Congress Cataloging-in-Publication Data

A catalog record has been applied for

To contact the author or translator:
BernardOffen@gmail.com; ngjacobs@msn.com

To contact the publisher: info@vmbooks.com

Research editor, footnotes, maps and photographs: Norman G. Jacobs
Computer manipulation of maps and graphics: Janis³awa Sitek

Printed by The Good News Press Ltd, Ongar, Essex

Contents

Part I From Kazimierz to the Ghetto, 1939–43

Part II Płaszów Concentration Camp and Julag Labor Camp, 1943–44

Part III Auschwitz and the Process of Healing, 1944–Present

List of Illustrations

Za wolność waszą i naszą ...

For your freedom and ours ...

A Polish motto, declared on Good Friday, 23 April 1943, by the Jewish Fighting Organization to the Polish people on behalf of the joint struggle of those in the Warsaw Ghetto and the Polish Underground Resistance Army.

For my brothers and sons, and for Krystyna Łapczyńska-Ryba, and to the memory of over fifty people in my family who perished due to the hatred of others; and to 'my angels' who, throughout my period in the ghetto and concentration camps, saved my life many, many times – by giving me an extra piece of bread or clothing, told me what to do, where to work, where to sleep – and so helped me to survive.

I have a debt to all these people: to witness. For those who took me under their wings did so as if I was their own child – maybe in the hope that someone else would help their families.

My task, the imperative to tell others what I witnessed, has been difficult. Having my life has been a gift. But it has also been a burden.

Survival, or just the fact of living, poses a challenge for us all: an opportunity to heal the wounds and traumas of others, as well as our own.

To all those who are on a similar journey, this book is also dedicated.

Bernard Offen
May 2007
Kraków, Poland

'For in much wisdom is much grief;
and he that increaseth knowledge increaseth sorrow.'
A Jewish proverb

The Library of Holocaust Testimonies

Ten years have passed since Frank Cass launched his Library of Holocaust Testimonies. It was greatly to his credit that this was done, and even more remarkable that it has continued and flourished. The memoirs of each survivor throw new light and cast new perspectives on the fate of the Jews of Europe during the Holocaust. No voice is too small or humble to be heard, no story so familiar that it fails to tell the reader something new, something hitherto unnoticed, something previously unknown.

Each new memoir adds to our knowledge not only of the Holocaust, but also of many aspects of the human condition that are universal and timeless: the power of evil and the courage of the oppressed; the cruelty of the bystanders and the heroism of those who sought to help, despite the risks; the part played by family and community; the question of who knew what and when; the responsibility of the wider world for the destructive behaviour of tyrants and their henchmen.

Fifty memoirs are already in print in the Library of Holocaust Testimonies, and several more are being published each year. In this way anyone interested in the Holocaust will be able to draw upon a rich seam of eyewitness accounts. They can also use another Vallentine Mitchell publication, the multi-volume *Holocaust Memoir Digest*, edited by Esther Goldberg, to explore the contents of survivor memoirs in a way that makes them particularly accessible to teachers and students alike.

Sir Martin Gilbert
London, April 2005

Acknowledgments

I would like to thank Danuta Grabowska, Agnieszka Osińska, Sister Violetta Reder, Richard Schlager, Ewa Struś and Karolina Wiśniewska for their assistance during my initial period of research. This involved creating transcriptions of Mr Offen's three films and interviewing the following people who kindly shared with me their memories of the Kraków Ghetto and Płaszów concentration camp: Miriam Akavia, Joseph Bossak, Meir Eldar, Leah Goodman, Stella Müller-Madej, Nathan Offen, Sam Offen, Dr Yael Peled, and Zdzisław Śmiłek.

Grateful acknowledgment is made to the following for their assistance: Mr Henryk Halkowski, Mr Władysław Klimczak (Director, Museum Historyczne Fotografii, Kraków), Dr Janusz Kurtyka (Instytut Pamięci Narodowej, Kraków), Mr Jan Piekło (Znak Christian Cultural Foundation), Dr Harald Schindler (Senior Historian, United States Holocaust Memorial Museum, Washington, DC), Dr Andrzej Szczygieł (Director, Muzeum Historyczne Miasta, Kraków), Ms Gołda Tencer (Fundacja Shalom, Warsaw), Dr Stefan Wilkanowicz (Znak Christian Cultural Foundation), Dr Jerzy Wróblewski (Director, Auschwitz Museum Archive, Oświęcim).

Special thanks, also, to Ms Barbara Berska (Archiwum Państwowe w Krakowie), Dyr. Eugeniusz Duda (Stara Bożnica, Kraków), Ms Hanna Pałuba (Fundacja Shalom, Warsaw), Mr Wacław Passowicz (Vice-Director, Muzeum Historyczne Miasta, Kraków), Mr Ken Schoen (Ken Schoen Books), Mr Tomasz Wroński and his colleagues (Instytut Pamięci Narodowej, Kraków), Mr Janusz Wysocki, and Mr Jarosław Żółciak.

Supportive people are important to any work of this nature and I thank in particular Katarzyna Jakubiak for her translation of *The Kraków Ghetto Song*; Łukasz Sakiewicz for contemporary photographs and his much valued help with overcoming the vagaries of my computer; Janisława Sitek for her painstaking work on maps and graphics; as well as Joel Cohen, Jolanta Dąbrowska, Agnieszka Drązszcz, Erin Einhorn, Dr Annamaria Orla-Bukowska, and Dr Gerry Silverman for their assistance in proofreading and suggesting improvements to the text.

Finally, I would like to thank Beata Rafflewska for her assistance and emotional support throughout the duration of this project.

Norman G. Jacobs
May 2007
Kraków, Poland

Foreword

At this time of year chestnuts fall from the trees in Kraków.
But no one any longer hangs them in a *sukkah*.
Wawel stands as it always has. But at the dragon's cave
There are no Jewish children.

The leaves cover the ground with a thick blanket
Near the University, as always a favorite meeting place for lovers.
But today the student corporations are not to be seen
And no one cries 'Beat the Jews', because there are no Jews.

The tower of the Virgin's Church still stands, so does the Sukiennice
And Mickiewicz still looks out over the Rynek.
The same houses, shops, churches and streets.
Only on Orzeszkowa you won't find *Nowy Dziennik*.

The dear pages of *Nowy Dziennik*,
The banner of Zion on the Kraków streets.
'Jerusalem' and 'the pogrom in Przytyk'
'Hitler' and 'The White Paper', 'Disturbances in Hebron'
and kosher slaughter and again politics,
And Bialik's poems translated by Dykman,
And an article by Dr Thon.

There is no more *Dziennik*, there are no more Jews
In Kazimierz the ghosts of the past still walk.
The Old Synagogue is falling down from age
And perhaps from sadness and shame ...

My Hometown Concentration Camp

On Józef street, on Ester, on Dietel
Jewish beggars no longer knock on the doors.
On Szeroka, Skawińska and Wąska
The wind howls and weeps.

From Wawel to Stradom
The tramway runs
Along Krakowska street.
Here you heard Yiddish,
Here you could smell Jewish sorrow,
Here were spread before you the Planty on Dietel street,
Here the Jewish holidays were celebrated
With the help of God.

At this time on Miodowa
A happy, festive, holiday crowd
Went to the Ajzyk synagogue, to Remu, to the Old Synagogue
And to the Tempel – the shrine of the progressive.
At this time in Kraków, you heard the yearning voice of the shofar
And the prayers of the faithful rose hopefully to heaven.

Today, there only remain
Desecrated scrolls
And Azkarot –
Memorial Services for the departed.

A memorial service for Stradom and for Kazimierz,
For Jakub street, for Józef, Szeroka, Miodowa,
For Rabbi Meisels street and for Podbrzezie,
For Orzeszkowa, Skawińska and for Brzozowa.

For those who raised the standard of revolt in the ghetto,
For our Jewish fighters – the soldiers of hope
Thrown like a stone by God against the ramparts
Thus they went in turn to their deaths
– for the memory of the Hebrew School
– for the theatre on Bocheńska
– for years, months, weeks and days.

– for the whole of Jewish Kraków
– for Mizrachi and Beis Yaakov
– for Maccabi and the Jewish Gymnastic Club.

Where is Kraków? Where is the Vistula? What has happened to us?
'Where is Rome, where Crimea and where Poland?'
Our Kraków stretches for many kilometers
from Płaszów to the Urals, to Sverdlovsk.
From Auschwitz to Siberia it accompanies us
To Paris, London, New York, to all corners of the world
And we who still survive after so much, after so many years
We gather and we remember, we gather and we remember.

We gather like the chestnuts on the Planty of Kraków
We thread a chain of memory longer than slavery;
Our idyllic Kraków Jewish childhood,
Days of struggle and exaltation, days youth and pranks,
Days of love, days of happiness, days of disaster, days of sadness.
Who knows as well as you, you Kraków streets,
What once pained us, what still pains us –
Our Jewish fate.

At this season, the chestnut trees are wet from the rain in Kraków
It is already autumn on the Planty and winter in our hearts
Darkness falls. It is time to return. The gates are closing.
It is slipping away, my unforgettable Kraków,
That Kraków which is no more.

'Kraków Autumn'
Natan Gross

Bernard Offen is one of three members of his large family who survived the Holocaust. Like many Kraków Jews, he feels a nostalgia for that 'unforgettable Kraków' described in the poem 'Krakow Autumn', written by another survivor from Kraków, Natan Gross. Kraków seems to have been an exception among Polish cities. Anti-Semitism was less acute here and the majority of Jews spoke Polish and felt a strong affinity to Polish culture, while also preserving their Jewish identity. Like other Kraków Jews who survived the war – one thinks in the first instance of the Rafael Scharf – Bernard Offen feels a strong impulse to explain Poles to Jews and Jews to Poles, insofar as these are clearly differentiated categories. He was sixteen when the war ended, having experienced the hell of the ghetto in the Podgórze area of Kraków and the concentration camps of Płaszów, Julag, Mauthausen, Auschwitz-Birkenau and Dachau-Kaufering. After the war he settled in the United States and in 1981 he went back to Poland for the first time. Since 1991 he has been a regular visitor to Kraków. He has made a series of documentary films dealing with the Holocaust: *The Work* (1983); *My Hometown Concentration Camp* (1997, also the title of this book); *Process B-7815: Hawaii and the Holocaust* (2003) and *Return to Auschwitz* (2007). He has also guided over 5,000 people through the scenes of his childhood and his wartime experiences. His goal, as he puts it, is through 'an account of my journey from a numbness built on fear to personal trust' to encourage 'self-reflective examination of individual beliefs and doubts' which he hopes will lead to 'greater relationships, moral compassion and, perhaps, a gain in understanding and love between human beings'.

This goal is also reflected in his moving memoir. There have been many first-hand accounts of the life of Jews in Kraków during the Second World War. They include the collection of memoirs and documents edited by Michał Borwicz and others under the title *W 3-cią rocznicę zagłady ghetta w Krakowie* (1946), Bertha Ferderber-Salz's memoir, *And the Sun Kept Shining* (1980), Bronisław Szatyn's memoir, translated into English under the title *A Private War: Surviving in Poland on False Papers* (1985), the English translation of Arieh Bauminger's *The Fighters of the Cracow Ghetto* (1986), Alexander Bieberstein, *Zagłada Żydów w Krakowie* (1986), Stanisław Dobrowolski's account of his activities in the Kraków branch of Żegota, *Memuary pacyfisty* (1989) and Malvina Graf's memoir, *The Kraków Ghetto and the Płaszów Camp Remembered* (1989).

Many have been published since the end of communism in Poland, including Irena Bronner's memoir, *Cykady nad Wisłą i Jordanem* (1991), the moving account of their work in Żegota by Miriam Peleg-Mariańska and Mordecai Peleg entitled *Witnesses: Life in Occupied Kraków* (1991), Gusta Dawidsohn Draenger's memoir of the Jewish resistance in Kraków, translated into English as *Justyna's Narrative* (1996), Halina Nelken's memoir, translated into English as *And yet, I am here!* (1999) and that of Natan Gross, translated into English as *Who are you, Mr Grymek?* (2001).

What makes Bernard Offen's account unique is the way he intersperses his description of what was done to the Jews with his account of what one can see in the same places today, an account which draws heavily on his own experience guiding groups around these sites of suffering and martyrdom. He also gives an account of how he came to terms with the trauma he suffered and became a convinced believer in reconciliation. It is this which makes his book not only a moving testimony but an essential companion for those many tourists visiting Kraków today who want to relive the experience of its Jews during the Holocaust and who want to understand the wider significance of this experience. They can have no better guide than Bernard Offen and I most warmly welcome the publication of his book.

Antony Polonsky
July 2007

Preface

Jewish and Christian relations in Polish history

Jewish life in Poland dates back to before the eleventh century.[1] The natural increase of the country's Jewish population had risen so that by 1939, nearly 10 per cent of the country's population was Jewish: an estimated 3.3 million Jews out of a total population of around 36 million people.[2]

Maintaining contrary beliefs and attitudes to the fervently Catholic majority, the Jews of Poland were a markedly separate community; both Catholics and Jews tended to view their neighbours from perspectives shaped and influenced by their traditional religious convictions.

The notion of the Jews as a 'wandering people,' exiled from their historical homeland, consequently supported the conception of Jews as eternal foreigners. Jews were, hence, commonly regarded as secondary citizens, *goście*, or guests, by many Christian Poles. Similarly, both the Judaic notion of the Gentile and the Christian concept of the infidel Jew acted as means of segregation and separation between the two communities, strengthening old communal resentments and influencing day-to-day perceptions.

In effect, each group saw the other not only as undifferentiated (either 'Christian' or 'Jew'), but as *morally and spiritually inferior* to their self-projected image of *superiority*.[3]

Although continual friction existed between Christians and Jews, Polish Jews were by no means monolithic in their own civil attitudes or religious and political views. During the nineteenth century, a split occurred in Poland between Jews who remained Orthodox, or Hassidic, and others who, influenced by the German Enlightenment, altered their beliefs in line with the *Haskalah* or other religious reform movements. Some Jews adapted via cultural and intellectual assimilation. Still others, a marginal few, converted to Christianity. This shift continued so that, by the 1930s, although many of Kraków's Jews were nominally Orthodox, around 60 per cent of the local Jewish population was largely acculturated in terms of education.[4] Hassidic Jews comprised a very small minority. The first three decades of the twentieth century saw a large advance toward modernity through support of one of two new movements: the religious-socialist *Histachdrut* Zionist movement – the *Rosh Pinna* organization existed in Kraków from 1883 – and the Bundist socialists.

Whereas Zionism promoted the spoken Hebrew language and a return to the Promised Land, Bundism emphasized Yiddish and the need for Jewish workers to integrate with others but still maintain their separate ethnic cultural values and identity. A fierce contest emerged between the Zionist and Bundist socialists. Although some interest rose in the Zionist movement, particularly after the First Zionist Congress in Basel in 1897, Kraków's Jews showed more interest in the Bundist socialist movement. Following the Holocaust, however, and the creation of a Jewish state, Bundism became an almost entirely forsaken ideology, replaced by a fervently nationalist Zionism.

The years 1918–39

The rebirth of a Polish state, following the Treaty of Versailles, triggered the development of a large number of political parties and splinter groups. Some political parties openly supported anti-Jewish legislation.

The right-wing National Democratic Party (*Endecja*), founded by Roman Dmowski, opposed the large percentage of Jewish professionals in Polish society. Although Polish national hero Józef Piłsudski called right-wing anti-Semitism 'the poisoning of the nation's soul',[5] *Endecja* became one of the largest and most popular political parties in Poland. Such an ethnically biased political climate also inhibited favourable ties between Jewish and non-Jewish socialist movements,[6] even though they did exist.

Along with most of the rest of Europe, Poland suffered the effects of global depression after the Wall Street stock market crash in New York in 1929. Although the National Democrats had somewhat limited power during Piłsudski's years of leadership from 1926 to 1935, following his death they used the economic situation to their political advantage. They, like other right-wing political parties, blamed wealthy Jewish traders, all minorities, and every 'foreigner' for a situation that affected both Jews and Poles and, in reality, was in no one's hands.[7]

Having caught the attention of the popular (that is, non-Jewish) vote, a number of large Jewish-owned businesses were nationalized in the late 1930s, and other restrictions – including the prohibition of ritual slaughter of animals, and working on Sundays – were made against Poland's Jewish population. Unassimilated Jews were forbidden to work in the civil service and in the army. In the previous decade, quotas had been enforced for a while, restricting many prospective Jewish students from entering some Polish universities since, according to the government, too high a proportion of students were Jewish; in the previous decade, 25 per cent of Kraków's college students had a Jewish background.

Separate benches for Jews and non-Jews existed from 1937 in some Polish universities. These were called 'bench ghettos'. The anti-Semitic atmosphere of 1930s Europe was a major contributing factor to the genocidal social policy that the Third Reich planned and carried out.[8]

In the two decades of the Polish Republic, a series of opposing trends existed side by side. Since opinion concerning Jews was mixed, it would be misguided to generalize about Polish attitudes toward Jews and anti-Semitism. There was no one overriding uniform view. Unlike Germany, which enforced its Nuremberg Laws in the years preceding the war, Poland could boast strong democratic political opposition to anti-Semitism.[9]

During the war, feelings about Jews were largely influenced by local events. One major curiosity of this period is that while Jews were victimized by Poles in one town, they were saved by Poles in another. Where inter-communal conflict did occur, it was often the result of concentrated efforts (as anti-Polish as they were anti-Semitic) by the Germans and the Soviets; propaganda was responsible for fomenting traditional resentments, presenting testimony and 'facts' based on obscure, and often falsified, historical sources in order to heap blame on Jews for circumstances that their enemies had created.[10] The Germans were responsible for burning a synagogue in Łódź and then blaming the Poles for doing it; the Germans explained that this was an angry Polish response to the alleged desecration earlier of a statue of Kościuszko. The Germans, of course, were really responsible for the destruction of the Kościuszko statue.[11]

The Second World War: The occupation of Poland and the destruction of European Jewry

On 12 October 1939, six weeks after marching across Poland and launching the first shots of the Second World War, Adolf Hitler annexed the western and north-eastern lands of Poland, adding them to the expanding Reich. The rest of the country – comprising the four districts of Warsaw, Kraków, Lublin and Radom – constituted a separate occupied territory, the *Generalgouvernement*. This was ruled by Hitler's former lawyer, Dr Hans Frank, from Kraków's Wawel Castle and Frank's palatial home in Przegorzały, a hamlet five kilometers outside the city.

In the first year of occupation, Frank oversaw the initial victimization of political enemies, Polish intellectuals, clergymen, and aristocrats.[12] No less than 3,500 members of the Polish elite were either executed or sent to concentration camps.[13] Within a year, about 20,000 non-Jewish Poles were taken to concentration camps in Germany. On 6 November 1939, 183 professors from Kraków's Jagiellonian University were arrested and sent to the Sachsenhausen concentration camp in Germany. Forty priests were executed and numerous others relocated. These acts and other killings were designed to terrorize and subdue civilian resistance, while effectively removing leadership from Polish society.

Destroying central Poland's governmental, economic, and educational infrastructure provided the Nazis with a malleable and highly serviceable vassal nation.

Stages of the Holocaust
The Holocaust of European Jews in Poland took place in three specific stages: (i) the initial stage of the occupation, (ii) the ghetto period, from 1941, (iii) the commencement and realization of the Final Solution, begun in 1942.

In Kraków, between September 1939 and March 1941 – the first stage of the Holocaust – Nazi powers deprived the city's almost 70,000 Jews of their commercial and civil rights while methodically separating the Jewish community from the rest of Polish society through a number of mobility restrictions. Jews, identifiable by the wearing of a white armband marked with a blue Star of David, from November 1939, were assigned forced labour tasks.

Prior to the war, Kraków had the fourth largest Jewish population in Poland. Warsaw had the country's greatest Jewish population of around 350,000 – 40 per cent of its total population – followed by Łódź and Lwów. (For details of Kraków's population growth in the first decades of the century, see Appendix.) Forced displacement and movement of Jews to other towns and cities meant that out of a total registered population of 68,482, only about 16,000 Jews remained in Kraków after the first year of the occupation.

Initially, many Jews left the cities for more rural areas. The start of the second stage, however, the ghetto period, from 1941, saw the forced concentration of all of Poland's Jews into small enclaves just outside city centres, for the dual purpose of utilizing forced labour and isolating Jews from other Poles. In Kraków, the remaining few thousand of the city's ghetto Jews were sent to Płaszów camp in 1943 where they, Polish-

Christian prisoners, and Jews from other ghettos across Poland, continued to labour under starvation conditions.[14]

The third stage, the so-called Final Solution, decided at the 1942 Wannsee Conference, began with the *Aktion Reinhardt* deportations of Jewish ghetto inhabitants to extermination camps; this included two transports in 1942 of approximately 6,000 and 4,500 people from the Kraków Ghetto to Bełżec extermination camp. The next step saw the liquidation of all the ghettos, with prisoners either sent to labour or concentration camps, or murdered if considered either too old or unfit to work.[15]

Following Germany's occupation of Hungary in 1944, the population of Płaszów concentration camp was supplemented by an influx of Slovakian and Hungarian Jews in transit to extermination at Auschwitz. As the war came to a close, the destruction of European Jewry carried on relentlessly.

Plans for the 'Final Solution'
As Reinhardt Heydrich stated at the conference in Berlin on 21 September 1939, plans for the Jewish population of Europe were already in place:

> In reference to today's conference in Berlin, I once again draw your attention to the fact that the jointly planned actions [the Final Solution] must be kept strictly a secret. You should differentiate the final solution (which will take a longer time) from the stages leading to that final solution (which will be realized in short periods of time). [...] The first foundation leading to the final solution is concentrating Jews from the provinces in bigger towns ... In each Jewish community a Jewish Council of the Seniors should be established ... The Council should be charged with all the responsibility, in the full sense of the word, for the precise execution of all orders ...[16]

Manipulation, exploitation and systematic handling of the Jewish ghetto population was conducted through Nazi control of the *Judenrat* (Jewish Council), helping to limit suspicion and assisting to manufacture a degree of consensus to German plans within the ghetto.

Dr Artur Rosenzweig, the president of the Kraków Ghetto *Judenrat*, did not acquiesce and follow Nazi orders. As a result, Dr Rosenzweig was sent, along with his entire family, on the June 1942 transport from the ghetto, probably to an extermination camp. He was replaced by Dawid Guter.[17]

In late 1941, Frank sent his deputy, State Secretary Dr Joseph Bühler, to Berlin to the first conference specifically on the Final Solution. By this time, Frank had already begun negotiations with officials in Berlin to 'resettle' the Jews to the east.

Shortly afterwards, on 16 December 1941, Frank and other officials met in Kraków. Frank stated: 'I want to say to you quite openly that we shall have to finish with the Jews, one way or another', for if Jewry survived the war, then, he reasoned, Germany's victory would be in vain. Consequently, the Jews had to disappear. 'Certainly', said Frank, 'a major migration is about to start. But what is to happen to the Jews? Do you think they will actually be resettled in Ostland villages? ... We have to annihilate the Jews wherever we find them and wherever it is at all possible.'[18]

The task of annihilation, Frank explained, would be accomplished without judges and courts. This *Aktion* would involve killing-installations established on occupied Polish territory. 'Resettlement' of Jews toward 'the east' would begin, with Poland as headquarters for the extermination of European Jewry.

After the war

The Second World War claimed 5 million Polish lives: 2 million Christians, 3 million Jews.[19]

In the first years after the war it was estimated that Kraków's Jewish community numbered around 6,000, mostly Jews from other parts of Poland and about 2,000 of the city's 70,000 former Jewish inhabitants. It is calculated that the Holocaust resulted in a loss to Kraków's pre-war Jewish population of over 86 per cent.[20]

This figure decreased in the ensuing years due to a variety of events. Following the first months after the war, which saw pogroms in Kielce and Kraków,[21] three waves of emigration occurred. In 1948, many Jews who had not already found refuge in other countries went to the newly founded State of Israel, and in 1956 and 1968, the Soviet authorities in Russia approved and sanctioned 'nationalist' acts of anti-Semitic propaganda against Poland's already small Jewish minority.

The year 1956 saw the officially-declared end of the Stalinist years of communist rule. The new era, with Poland under the leadership of Władysław Gomułka, swiftly saw a settling of previous wrongs – 'Stalinist measures' – with the removal of Jakub Berman, chief of the country's Communist Security Police (1952–56) during the era of Poland's former president, Bolesław Bierut. Berman was of Jewish origin. He and other 'Muscovites' – the term used to refer to Polish Communist Jews – were expelled from the Communist Party between 1956 and 1957 as the party underwent internal reorganization.

Described as a criminal by Władysław Szpillman, in his book *The Pianist* (made into a film by Roman Polański), Berman was one of Stalin's puppets and was directly responsible for ordering some atrocious incidents. Unfortunately, there followed an immediate backlash of Soviet-inspired nationalism, which was anti-Semitic in content.

Although dissent had reached a new level, the reform that supposedly took place was quite short-lived. The Soviet Party apparatus' hold on power, and opposition to political and social freedoms across the Eastern bloc, remained of primary concern – displayed, not least, in the fierce retributions following the failed Hungarian Revolution.

Many still blame Gomułka, who led the country from 1956 to 1970, for the purges and the increased pressure on Jews to leave Poland. In contrast to the Soviet leadership, however, Gomułka granted Jews the necessary documents to leave Poland. Nonetheless, abroad, Polish anti-Semitism appeared inextricable from the entire situation in Eastern Europe, which had not been particularly sympathetic to the plight of Jews since the war.

The period 1967–68 saw a mass of political and social movement action across the globe. French students went on strike and brought France close to civil war. American social discontent grew in the same year that Martin Luther King and Bobby Kennedy were both assassinated.

In Poland, at a time of economic crisis, and when the Soviets were verbally attacking Israel, aiming to curry favour with oil-rich Arab nations, right-wing nationalist Mieczysław Moczar made a similarly fuelled attack, replete with anti-Jewish rhetoric. The foremost reason behind this attack was his objective of ousting Gomułka from leadership. Although his attempt ultimately failed, a greater tragedy befell Poland's remaining Jewish population as this new internal power struggle was played out. At least 20,000 Polish Jews were pressured into leaving the country, with the effect that, according to Norman Davies, 'Poland's Jewish community shrank from about 30,000 to perhaps 5,000.'[22] The remaining Jewish community comprised mostly elderly people. This may account for the gradual recorded decrease in Kraków's Jewish population, from 600 in 1978 to less than 200 in 2001.[23]

Historians Jerzy Lukowski and Hubert Zawadzki write:

> Led by Mieczysław Moczar, the deputy minister of the interior [and a personally motivated rival to Gomułka for the Party leadership], the so-called 'Partisans' espoused a crude nationalism that was anti-German, anti-Ukrainian and anti-Semitic. They targeted liberalizing pro-reformers within the Party [including Jacek Kuroń, historian Dr Karol Modzelewski and former dissident Adam Michnik], as well as 'cosmopolitan' writers and film-makers ... The condemnation of Israel and Zionism by the USSR and most of its east European satellites during the Arab–Israeli war of June 1967 was not shared by Poland's small number of Jews or indeed by many young Poles. Gomułka personally had no record of anti-

Semitism (and his wife was of Jewish origin), but his public condemnation of Polish 'Zionists' who had rejoiced in Israel's victory as a potential 'fifth column' provided an excellent opportunity for Moczar and his followers to exploit anti-Semitism in their bid for power. In a climate of political hysteria, tantamount to a witch-hunt, all Party members of Jewish origin were expelled from their posts ...[24]

Subsequent to March 1968, the phenomenon of 'anti-Semitism without Jews' occurred from time to time in Poland. A mixture of old stereotyped images to be used in time of political and social distress, this phenomenon remains up to and including the present; at election time, opposition often appears in the form of graffiti declaring that a candidate is Jewish.

Fortunately, however, actual incidents of anti-Semitism have started to wane. Although one may sceptically assess that pro-Semitism, the flip side of the country's old prejudices, exists instead, especially among the younger generation of Poles, it is true that several major improvements have occurred. These, in education and across the majority of media channels, seem to be a result of the changes taking place as Poland is further integrated within the new post-Communist European framework.

Rescue of Jews: momentary, temporary and sustained

During the war, the fate of individual Jews was considerably affected by one or more of several factors. Jews were able at times to escape detection if they had managed to gain false identity documents, especially if they had Aryan or non-Jewish features. Although, as Emmanuel Ringelblum wrote in his Warsaw Ghetto diary, 'There were Jews with a first-rate Aryan appearance who did not speak Polish well or had a noticeable accent, people who could not even pronounce their Aryan name correctly.'[25] Jews who spoke only Yiddish, or had a 'Jewish accent,' were discovered and apprehended almost without exception.[26] The Jews who managed to escape were those who were sufficiently polonized to be able to convey the impression that they were Catholic Poles. A few Jews managed to maintain this identity throughout the war, even while in concentration camps.[27] At the same time, much of the Jewish intelligentsia, perhaps the most assimilated sub-group of Polish Jewry, had been executed along with their non-Jewish counterparts in the first year of the war.[28]

Jews always faced the possibility of being caught by a German soldier, or a Ukrainian or Latvian guard under the command of the Nazis. Some Poles, including even a few Jews, acted as informers for the Nazis. The number of *szmalcownik*, or scum, was not inconsiderable. As Władysław Bartoszewski[29] writes:

> At the same time we were saving Jews, we were trying to prosecute Polish and Jewish collaborators who blackmailed the families hiding Jews and the Jews themselves. In some cases our colleagues working in the appropriate sections of the underground had to pass death sentences. They had to execute them. There was no other way out: those blackmailers were a deadly threat in that situation – both for Jews and for Poles.[30]

Nevertheless, good people did exist who acted courageously in assisting Jews. Zofia Kossak-Szczucka, co-founder of *Żegota*[31] and a leading activist of the Catholic Front for the Rebirth of Poland, made the following statement:

> The world is looking at [a] crime, which is more outrageous than anything in its history and remains silent. The massacre of the millions of helpless people takes place amidst the general, ominous silence that can no longer be tolerated. Whatever its reasons, it is just dishonorable. In the face of a crime one cannot be passive. One who remains silent in the face of a murder becomes an accomplice of the murderers. One who does

not condemn it, lets it happen.[32]

At the same time, Kossak-Szczucka repeated the old accusation that Jews were an economic enemy of Poland: one example of what Ewa Hoffman calls the unfortunate 'cognitive disjuncture' between how some Poles think and feel about Jews.

Nonetheless, many non-Jewish Poles sacrificed their own lives helping Jews, knowing the fate that they risked if caught: Poland was the only occupied country where the death penalty was automatically imposed upon those who assisted Jews.[33] The Association of Former Political Prisoners estimates the number of Poles murdered for helping Jews at 2,500.[34] This figure could however be much higher, up to 50,000.[35]

Among these were Catholic nuns and priests who, under no direction other than their own consciences, assisted Jewish children by harbouring them in their convents and monasteries. Most were girls, since young Jewish boys were easily detected during Nazi inspections (usually having been circumcised), and would have put the other convent child refugees at risk.[36] According to Ewa Kurek's study, approximately 1,200 Jewish children were housed in 189 convents during the war.[37] Seven convents rescued Jewish children in Kraków alone.[38]

Even so, raids on convents and churches often led to the discovery and consequent sending of Jewish children to concentration camps, as well as potentially punishment for all those with knowledge that the children were Jewish. In one account, Holocaust survivor Anita Lobel writes of being sent with her brother to Płaszów concentration camp along with several other Jewish children following a round-up during a traditional Christmas Day church service in 1944.[39]

For a few more fortunate individuals, sustained rescue lasted throughout the war.[40] Though, for the majority of Jews saved through the efforts of others – usually Poles they knew personally – rescue was only temporary: from a week to several months.

For the young Bernard Offen, momentary reprieve was the single merciful night when, in the midst of the war, the

Catholic Cieślik family cared for him at their home in Kraków Podgórze. Although for just one night, and at considerable risk to themselves, he recalls that it made an enormous difference, even though uncertainty and the risk of annihilation constantly surrounded him.

Apart from those few hours, he suffered the entirety of the Holocaust in either a ghetto, or a labor, concentration or death camp. Some child survivors of the concentration camps owe their lives to the fact that their parents served as engineers or *Ordnungsdienst* officers and gained occasional privileges – food rations or the promise that their children would be kept with them in the camp. Others survived by working at Oskar Schindler's factory or being added to his transport to eventual freedom. Bernard Offen did not have any of these advantages.

Reading his story, one is reminded again and again that Mr Offen's life was spared due to a mixture of chance plus one simple ingredient: compassion. His family's love, care from one Christian family, the support of other prisoners, and his personal willpower helped him to endure all the punishments and hardships of the concentration camp universe. Consequently, though historians, psychologists and sociologists continue to deliberate why Nazis, or any totalitarian body, can quickly turn apparently ordinary men into obedient killing machines, if Mr Offen's experiences are to have any meaning today, then we, contemporary ordinary men and women, should heed the lessons from the millions who died in the Holocaust through refusing to allow brutalities and atrocities to take place now.

Norman G. Jacobs
May 2007
Kraków, Poland

NOTES

1. Jews first settled in Kraków in the thirteenth century.
2. See Appendix. According to different historians, estimates of the number of Polish Jewish survivors range from 50,000 to 200,000. Lukas (1997), p. 149.
3. Hundert (1992).
4. Duda (1991), p. 138. Lukas states that 'most of the three million Jews who lived in Poland were unassimilated'. Lukas (1997), p. 121. 'Emancipated assimilationism was a strong trend in Poland.' Miłosz (2000), p. 30.
5. Korboński (1989), p. 130.
6. Gross (2001), p. 291, footnote 7.
7. Czesław Miłosz writes: 'Only the ... economic crisis provided the nationalists with the right conditions. I have to add that they had the majority of the Catholic clergy behind them. One particular phenomenon was the mass-circulation press published by the Franciscan fathers Niepokalanów [near Warsaw], especially the newspaper called *May Dziennik*, which specialized in anti-Semitic propaganda. It found a wide response among Polish villagers and small-town dwellers, resulting in attacks on Jewish market stalls, the destruction of Jewish property, and a boycott on Jewish shops.' Miłosz (2000), p. 30.
8. Fritz Stern writes: ' [S]cholars have now established that both Germans and non-Germans knew far more far earlier about the Holocaust than was once assumed. But most of these people worried about their own predicaments and tried to preserve their own complacent self-regard, their moral self-esteem, by choosing not to know or believe – a denial that has marked most of the world in our century.' Stern (2001), p.285. For further reference to this issue see Korboński, pp. 53–4 and p. 106 (on evidence that the Allies knew about Nazi genocidal policy); Hilberg (1985), pp. 324–31 (on the Eichmann initiative); Breitman (1998).
9. Lukas (1997), p. 126.
10. Popular historical consciousness of Polish–Jewish wartime relations has been much shaped by film, television and the media, which tend to focus on single incidents of Polish anti-Semitism. This, arguably, may result in a lessening of a wider understanding of Polish–Jewish relations during the war, media consciousness itself being commonly influenced by 'local' political biases.
11. Emmanuel Ringelblum quoted in Lukas (1997), p.128.
12. On 19 September 1939, Security Police Chief Heydrich met with *Generalquartiermeister* Wagner of the Army High Command to discuss some Polish problems. The two officials agreed upon 'a clean up once and for all' of 'Jews, intelligentsia, clergy, nobility'. Hilberg (1985), p. 65.
13. Mayer (1988), pp. 184–5.
14. Daily food allotment to Varsovians in 1941 was 669 calories to Poles, 184 to Jews, 2,613 to Germans. Lukas (1997), p.30.
15. Non-Jews continued to be sent to concentration camps. From 1942 to 1944 existed the Liban camp, located 200 to 300 metres from Płaszów concentration camp. About 2,000 prisoners were processed during its existence. Named after the company's owner, Liban camp workers were mostly captured escapees from the *Baudienst* building service. Working conditions in the camp's stone quarry were severe, and brutal guards governed the camp. Wroński (1981b).
16. From *Eksterminacja Żydów na ziemach polskich w okresie okupacji hitlerowskiej: zbior dokumentów* (*The Extermination of Jews in Poland during the German Occupation: A collection of documents*), Żydowski Instytut Historyczny, Warsaw, 1957, p. 26: quoted in Kurek (1997), p. 18.
17. Graf (1989), p. 44. Guter collaborated with the Nazis but, like Symche Spira, paid with his life at Płaszów. Pankiewicz (1985).
18. Hilberg (1985), pp. 187–8.

19. According to a report made in 1947, 6,028,000 Polish citizens lost their lives in the war: 22 per cent of the country's population, making the highest ratio of losses to population of any country in Europe. Lukas (1997), p. 38. Today, scholars of independent Poland believe that 1.8 to 1.9 million Polish civilians (non-Jews) were victims of German occupation policies and the war. Information from United States Holocaust Memorial Museum publication, *Poles*.
20. This figure includes those who survived but did not return, probably a few hundred.
21. The Kraków pogrom took place in September 1945. Twenty-two Jews were murdered by non-Jewish locals. Cichopek (2000).
22. Davies and Moorhouse (2002), p. 478.
23. Figures refer to those registered with the Kraków Jewish Community.
24. Lukowski and Zawadzki (2001), pp. 265–6.
25. Ringelblum quoted in Kurek (1997), p. 32.
26. In the national census of 1931, close to 80 per cent of the Jews declared Yiddish to be their mother tongue. Lukas (1997), p. 123.
27. See Taubenschlag (1998).
28. Lukas (1997), p. 144.
29. Member of Poland's Home Army and more recently the Foreign Minister.
30. From *Warto być uczciwym ...* quoted in Kurek (1997), p. 48.
31. For further information on *Żegota* see Lukas (1997), pp. 147–151 and 287–309.
32. Duda (1999), p. 72.
33. Frank had stated, on 15 October 1941, the *Ogoszenie*, declaring the penalty of death awaiting those Poles who attempted to assist Jews who tried to escape. A second similar warning was made a year later as Poles continued with their assistance to Jews (25 October 1941): 'Jews who leave their designated districts are subject to the penalty of death. The same penalty will be applied to persons who knowingly provide shelter for such Jews.' Similarly, on 28 September 1942, a declaration by the German Commissioner of Ostrowiec, Motschall, reminded all Poles: 'In view of the repeated instances of Jews being hidden by Poles ... anyone who shelters Jews and gives or sells them food will be punished by death.' Korboński (1987), p. 43.
34. Ibid., p. 67.
35. See Lukas (1997), pp. 310–39.
36. The rescue of Jewish children by the Church is a subject that evokes intense emotions to this day, owing to the attitude of both Christians and Jews at the time. Nahum Bogner (2000), p. 1, writes:

> The Jewish collective consciousness associates the affair with the conversion of many of these children to Christianity – as if their rescuers effected their deliverance in order to stalk innocent souls and exploit their existential distress for missionary motives. Christians, in contrast, consider the very hint of such a suspicion as an expression of ingratitude on the part of people who do not respect the death-defying devotion and Christian conscience of those priests and nuns who risked their lives in order to save Jews.

37. Kurek (1997), pp. 102–3.
38. Ibid., p. 109.
39. Lobel (1998).
40. Jews were helped by Poles more than in any other occupied nation: approximately 6,000 Christian Poles have been awarded the Medal of Honor by Israel's Yad Vashem Holocaust Memorial Center.

Introduction: A Journey of Healing

My story begins years after the Holocaust, after my enslavement in Nazi death camps. It begins not in Poland, but in the United States. It begins with my determination and first inner efforts to remember and to feel: to emotionally confront my memories and the feelings generated from them that I had repressed for many years. For thirty-six years I pressed my pains and fears down. Even to myself I denied what had happened to me and my family, as if it were all a dream. But, encouraged by the survivors who had spoken out before me, I began to imagine that I did not have to hide my experience of the Holocaust. I began to ask myself questions: What shall I do with my experience on this planet? How can I help so that others will not suffer the fate of my family and myself? How can I help others today?

I was born in Kraków in 1929. When the German army invaded Poland in September 1939, I was not yet 11 years old. In the following years until the end of the war, I experienced the conditions of the ghetto in Kraków and the concentration camps of Płaszów (pronounced *Pwa-shuf*), Julag, Mauthausen, Auschwitz-Birkenau, and Dachau-Kaufering.

My parents' names were Jacob and Rochme Gitel. In my family, over fifty people were murdered and only three survived: my two older brothers and I.

In 1981, I returned to Poland for the first time. For the past twenty years, since the fall of Communism, I have returned each year to the city of my birth. During these years, I have also made a trilogy of documentary films: *The Work* (1983), *My Hometown Concentration Camp* (1997), and *Process B-7815* (1999); and two further titles, *Hawaii and the Holocaust* (2003) and *Return to Auschwitz* (2007). I come to Krakw to witness and teach about my personal experience and about what Jewish life was like before the war. Walking with others, retracing the steps of my childhood, is for me part of a personal need to confront the past as well as part of a wider message – *of witnessing* – I wish to share with others.

Over five thousand people have walked with me in the area in which my family and I once lived but which became the place where the beautiful and glorious Jewish life of the Greater Kraków area, a 'Paris of the East', was ultimately destroyed. Where once there was a Jewish community of 65,000, there is a remnant now of less than 200, mostly older people.

To heal and to become whole, I have chosen to look, to confront, and to re-examine all of my experiences. From this, I believe, we may learn and grow as human beings.

This is my evolving theory of health. This is the real story I have to tell. It is an account of my journey from a numbness built on fear to personal trust and of a life in which risk-taking and the self-reflective examination of individual beliefs and doubts can lead to greater relationships, moral compassion and, perhaps, a gain in understanding and love between human beings.

I devote my life to bringing this message to others. It is a shocking message and one that contains a cruel and frightening reality but, in my view, it is also a message of hope. The transition from Holocaust and trauma to hope and trust is not easy or painless: it takes time. But I tell my story in the hope that others may learn from my life and that we all may grow as a result of my story, a *guide* for a life which travels a different path from my own passage of return and healing: *a life that reaches beyond survival.*

As the father of two young men, I am deeply concerned for their lives in a world that continues to reflect the symptoms of dehumanisation that allowed a person such as Adolf Hitler to rise to power. We must examine how that came into being.

Once we recognize the need for change, there must be a conscious dedication to the process of change. In as meaningful a way as I can, I wish to express the longing I have for a peaceful world. I can no longer contain my past experience or my observations of a world today overshadowed by the threat of a global Auschwitz.

So let us now take off our blinders and continue – by looking together. My witnessing is an invitation to shift from the paralyses of fear and unconsciousness to an active consciousness: from apprehension and hopelessness to a peaceful co-creation for the future, for ourselves and for our children.

This is what I consider my *journey of healing*.

Following reading my story, my hope is that you will examine your life. And how your life is with your wife, your kids and the people you work for. Who do you enrich with your work, or what your money helps to produce? Because fifty years from now, what we unconsciously create today, someone is going to take pleasure in or suffer from its consequences.

Time is passing. Nothing can be done about what happened at the ghetto and Płaszów camp. Another monument can be added, but this is simply an acknowledgment. It does not change things fundamentally if it does not lead to us changing our minds and acting differently.

In the wake of all my experiences, I think that we need to raise our comprehension as human beings and as who we potentially are, instead of that narrow-mindedness that exists all around the world. We have to focus on what we should be doing, what we believe, so that we might discover who we really are.

I believe there are two kinds of light that we could see as human beings in the world. One is the positive, constructive light of reason, and our unity as human beings. The other is the negative, destructive light of nuclear explosion.

That's why my message for posterity, for the future, is this: There is a phrase used by computer programmers, and the acronym for it is GIGO – garbage in, garbage out. What we put in is what we get out.

In other words, what we believe is what we create. So we really need to examine what it is that we believe.

Thank you. Peace and *shalom* to you all.

PART I

From Kazimierz to the Ghetto, 1939–43

1 Now and then: Before and after the Germans arrived

Today, I am walking the streets of Kraków. The old buildings speak of a past, their drab, peeling facades a reminder of the once rich and colorful civilization that has gone forever …

I continue on. Now, I am by where the iron bridge to Podgórze once stood, the hills where my family lived: where I was born and was raised with my brothers, Sam and Nathan, and my sister Miriam.

This is where we used to play, where we went to school and where a whole other life existed, so different to the one I know now.

As I walk again and again around the streets, memories fill me.

In the journey that follows, you will see the houses and other buildings where my family and countless others lived for such a long time, but whose existence there was so suddenly and cruelly cut short by the arriving Nazi force. I hope you will learn from our journey some sense of what was once there, and feel a flicker of the strength of the old Jewish community that battled on resolutely in its final days of the ghetto period; and realise that, in Płaszów, though barely a sign exists to say what happened here, this is the place where so many innocent lives and souls were destroyed.

Shadows of the past begin to merge, and, in some ways, things look almost the same as once before. Only now everyone has gone. Jewish life has disappeared. Eradicated. Extinguished …

The occupation: September 1939
Before Podgórze became a ghetto, it was just an ordinary

3

1. 1930s Szeroka, Kazimierz (Witold Chromiński, courtesy of Mr J. Wysocki)

2. Szewska Street, off Main Market Square, Kraków
(Muzeum Historyczne Miasta Krakowa)

neighborhood, as it is now – a neighborhood where people live. The streets were full of life and activity. There were friends and neighbors everywhere ...

The German attack on Poland began on 1 September 1939. Although the Polish army went on fighting throughout the war, it was defeated by the immense force of the German army on 5 October, made worse by the Soviet army's subsequent invasion of eastern Poland on 17 September 1939.

Kraków was occupied from 6 September. SS *Gruppenführer* Reinhardt Heydrich's orders immediately forbade Jews to walk in the Planty greenbelt area around Kraków's main Market Square, or to use public transport. Jews had been living in Kraków for over 900 years; suddenly we were all *personae non gratae*. Other restrictions came into effect for the entire local population. Round-ups included everyone, not only Jews.[1]

The Beginning of the ghetto period: March 1941
After the first displacements, during 1940, about 16,000 out of a total registered population of 68,482 Jews in Kraków remained. At the time, Kraków had the fourth largest Jewish population in Poland[2] – the city's total population at that time was around 240,000.

My family's neighbourhood in Kraków Podgórze was surrounded by ten-foot-high [three meter] walls, barbed-wire fences and armed SS, Gestapo men or members of the blue-uniformed Polish police. This followed Kraków Regional Governor Otto Wächter's decision on 3 March 1941 to create a 'Jewish residential district' in the town.

Jewish protest
In a bid to quell the measures taken against Jews, Rabbi Shmuel Shmelke Kornitzer, together with Rabbi Shabti Rapaport and Mayer Friedrich, wrote to the leading Catholic priest of the city, Archbishop Adam Stefan Sapieha. They asked him to oppose the Nazi expulsion of Jews from Kraków to other towns. Their intervention, however, was useless and, subsequently the three rabbis were arrested and sent to

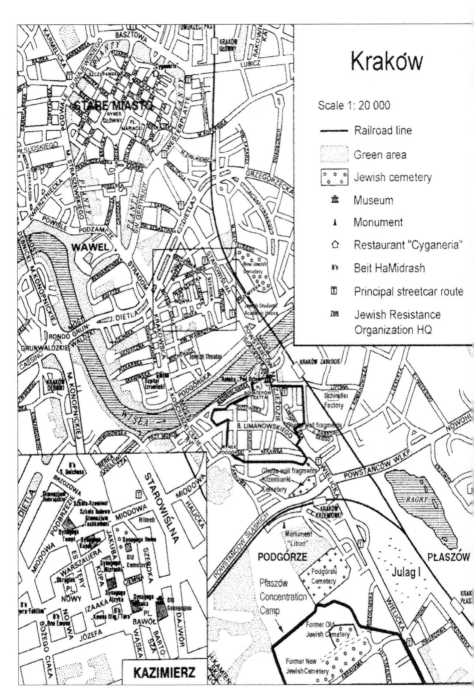

3. Map of Kraków (Jacobs/Sitek, from original in Duda (1991)

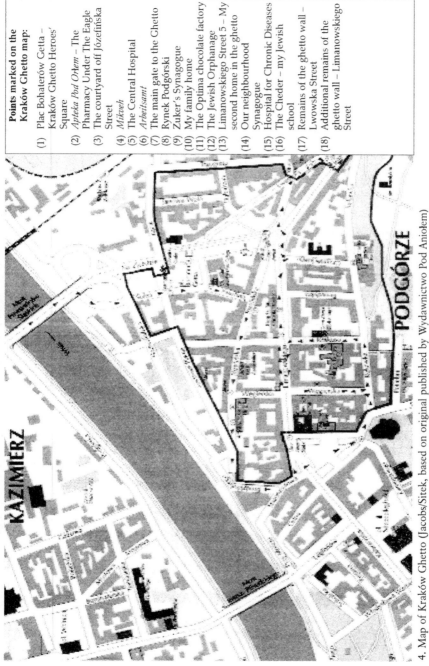

Points marked on the Kraków Ghetto map:

(1) Plac Bohaterów Getta – Kraków Ghetto Heroes' Square
(2) *Apteka Pod Orłem* – The Pharmacy Under The Eagle
(3) The courtyard off Józefińska Street
(4) *Mikveh*
(5) The Central Hospital
(6) *Arbeitsamt*
(7) The main gate to the Ghetto
(8) Rynek Podgórski
(9) Zuker's Synagogue
(10) My family home
(11) The Optima chocolate factory
(12) The Jewish Orphanage
(13) Limanowskiego Street 5 – My second home in the ghetto
(14) Our neighbourhood Synagogue
(15) Hospital for Chronic Diseases
(16) The Cheder – my Jewish school
(17) Remains of the ghetto wall – Lwowska Street
(18) Additional remains of the ghetto wall – Limanowskiego Street

4. Map of Kraków Ghetto (Jacobs/Sitek, based on original published by Wydawnictwo Pod Aniołem)

Auschwitz. None of them survived the Holocaust. In the Auschwitz Museum (Block 4) is displayed a copy of the telegram to Rabbi Kornitzer's wife informing her of the death of her husband, allegedly a victim of natural causes. They sent Rabbi Kornitzer's ashes back to Kraków, requesting payment for their shipment – a common Nazi practice to further insult and grieve the families of the people they had murdered.

Jews were forced to leave the old Jewish district of Kazimierz – 'for your protection from the anti-Semitic Poles', according to the Germans. The entire Jewish Quarter of Kraków was taken over by the Germans and 'Aryanized', something that included putting a brothel on Miodowa Street. Former residents were ordered to move across the river to the ghetto or other ghettos in Poland. This included the several hundred German Jews who had either left or been expelled from their homeland a few years earlier to escape the growing anti-Semitism there. Many people moved to rural villages, where they were safe, but only for a while. Most were either murdered or ghettoised in the subsequent year.

Although most of Kraków's Jews lived in the neighbouring districts of Kazimierz and Stradom, it would be wrong to think that these were the only areas where there were Jews. Jews owned houses in the Old Town, on central streets such as Grodzka, Bracka, Szewska, Floriańska, and Szpitalna. After 21 March 1941, however, having been given just a few days' notice, Jews were no longer permitted to live anywhere in Kraków outside the ghetto walls. On the day before the ghetto was sealed, much activity took place, people moving and carrying their possessions to the ghetto.

Later that year, around mid-October, Jews from the surrounding towns and villages in the Kraków area had to move to the ghetto. The Nazis spared themselves no amount of shame or callousness in choosing the holiest day in the Jewish calendar, Yom Kippur (the Day of Atonement), as the last day for entering the ghetto.

Inside the ghetto, 12,000 people had to live in buildings (there were around 320) which had previously been occupied

5. Forced transfer of Jews to the Kraków Ghetto, 1941 (United States Holocaust Memorial Museum)

6. Inside the Kraków Ghetto (Archiwum Państwowe w Krakowie)

by 3,500 residents. Often, several families – rich and poor, Orthodox and non-religious, Zionist or Bundist – had to live in the same apartment. The Germans considered one square meter adequate for each person. Following the move from the villages, the number of people living in the ghetto rose to around at least 16,000. It is estimated that later, by the autumn of 1941, with the liquidation of the local villages, there were 24,000 people in the ghetto. The rest of Kraków's Jews had, of course fled either to other cities or rural areas. Ultimately, however, most of them shared a fate similar to mine and that of the rest of my family.

Once in the ghetto, we were subjects of the Nazis, who were mass murderers and bandits on an unprecedented scale. One day, near the end of December 1941, an order went out through the ghetto for all fur coats and collars to be surrendered. Failure to do so would result in the usual penalty of execution. Death was the punishment for everything: for using public transportation, for not wearing the prescribed armband – or even having a fur coat. That's why people took their coats to the collection centre or threw them out into the street. Some simply cut them up and burned them in their house fires.

Five people were shot out on the street that day.[3]

In the ghetto, there were non-Jewish factories such as the Madritsch clothes factory, Optima workshops and Feliks Dziuba's optical glass works at Targowa Street 6. Just outside the ghetto, on Lipowa Street, was Oskar Schindler's factory which made enamelled pots and pans. Schindler's role in helping Jews is now well known, but Dziuba also helped Jews, employing people as 'specialists' who knew nothing at all about the work they were meant to do. Dziuba let them rest quietly during the day before they returned to the ghetto, but this lasted for only a short while. The Nazis were soon made aware of this practice by their informers – Poles who wanted to earn a little extra money, no matter how.

Each of the above businesses operated using Jewish slave laborers, made possible through their owner's contact with the SS. All Jewish businesses had been taken over by a *Treuhänder*.

Schindler was one such custodian, his factory having been owned by a Jew named Abraham Bankier.[4] This was how businesses and houses were dispossessed. Often the owners, once no longer needed to instruct the custodians how to operate the business, were sent to the camps and liquidated.

A few Jewish institutions remained in operation: hospitals, orphanages and care homes, and even a Jewish post office. To begin with, people were allowed to attend synagogue, to pray, fast and observe the religious holidays as much as they could – even if they still had to work on these days. The Germans, however, ordered restrictions on religious Jews through the closure of the three local synagogues. Eating kosher meat had been made impossible since the banning of the ritual slaughter of animals, following the German occupation, though this did not matter since there was no meat. Synagogues were desecrated, items being either destroyed or stolen – sometimes for the cause of the Reich, at other times simply sent to German soldiers' families. Religious teaching carried on but it was done largely in secret after the synagogues were closed down.

From the beginning, people in the ghetto were humiliated and beaten by the Germans. Shooting was called 'sport with the Jews'. I remember people being gunned down by guards if they tried to escape. The guards were laughing and enjoying this, as if they were just out hunting animals.

I remember fear and being humiliated verbally and physically. Hunger, disease and starvation were standard, part of normal life in the ghetto. I remember searching for scraps of food or fuel in garbage dumps and anywhere else I could find them. Surrounded by people dying from disease, this kind of life became ordinary. I think it was easier for children than adults.

Above all, my family still had hope. We prayed since my family was Orthodox. Even though I remember our having to wear an armband with a blue star, as if we were inferior human beings, we believed that things could not get worse. The war would end soon and surely God would save us.

11

From Kazimierz to Podgórze

Our walk starts from in front of the Old Synagogue, now a state museum for Polish Jewish Culture, dating from the fifteenth century – the oldest synagogue in Poland – on Szeroka Street 24 in Kazimierz (see Kraków Map on page 6). Following the map, go to Starowiślna Street going along the right hand side to reach the *Most Powstańców Śląskich* bridge. This spans across the River Wisła, bringing you into the district called Podgórze. The bridge you see now is not the original one that Jews from Kazimierz crossed to enter the ghetto. Most of the bridges in Kraków were destroyed by the Germans in January 1945, prior to the town's liberation.

Across the river, near the bridge, were some drainage outlets. It was through these that some people escaped from the ghetto via the sewers. This route was soon discovered by the Nazis who killed those they found trying to escape.

Turn right immediately past the bridge and go down the steps, keeping to the right as you follow the curving path. See Kraków Ghetto Map on page 7.[5]

(1) Plac Bohaterów Getta – Ghetto Heroes Square

Cross over to where you will see a shop, currently marked *Fryzjer*, on the corner of Nadwiślańska Street and Solna Street. Continue on past Piwna Street on the sidewalk of the square. At the adjacent corner building (Piwna Street 27), next to the Telepizza sign, is a wall-plaque naming the square in front Plac Bohaterów Getta, in memory of the efforts of resistance fighters and all other unnamed heroes from the ghetto. The *Żydowska Organizacja Bojowa* (*ŻOB* – Jewish Combat Organization) existed in addition to the Polish resistance. During the entire occupation, it used different forms of armed struggle against the German occupiers.[6] On 22 December 1942, several members of the *ŻOB* escaped the ghetto to carry out resistance attacks at places in the town centre frequented by the Nazis: Café Esplanada, the Skała cinema and the officers' casino in the National Museum. Several of these attacks had to be called

12

off for various reasons, but the planned grenade attack on *Restauracja Cyganeria*, Szpitalna Street 38 – across from the Sowackiego Theatre (a supermarket at the time of writing), was carried out, resulting in a number of SS men being either wounded or killed. The resistance fighters fled and returned to the ghetto, but, following a later firefight between resistance members and Nazi troops, almost all were caught, tortured and executed.

During the ghetto period the square served as the *Umschlagplatz* (Deportation Square). It was from here that most deportations of Kraków's Jewish citizens to the concentration camps began. Numerous times we were ordered to gather here, where we were often terrorized. And many, many were shot here.

(2) Apteka Pod Orłem – The Pharmacy Under The Eagle
On the corner of Targowa Street and Plac Bohaterów Getta is a museum (opened in 1983) dedicated to the ghetto and Płaszów concentration camp, *Apteka Pod Orłem*.[7] The pharmacy was managed by Tadeusz Pankiewicz, a Catholic man, and his three assistants. Officially, they dispensed medicines and basic aid to ghetto residents. Unofficially, the pharmacy acted as a shelter for some, as an underground conduit for the *ŻOB*, as well as a place for sending and receiving information. The pharmacy remained open for two-and-a-half years, from the beginning until the final liquidation of the ghetto, to maintain appearances, and because it was in the interests of the Nazis to keep out disease. The Nazis also took large bribes to keep it open.

After the war, Mr Pankiewicz wrote a powerful book – *Apteka w getcie krakowskim* – about his experiences during the ghetto period. In one recollection, Pankiewicz tells the story of *Hauptmann* Oswald Bousko, a Viennese man, assistant to the German police commander in Podgórze. Although he was one of the first Austrians to follow Hitler and join the SS, Bousko soon turned his back on Nazism. Bousko tried to help many Jews, while deceiving his compatriots. Threatened with having to join the battle at the eastern front, Bousko attempted to escape and for a time was successful. He was caught, however, and imprisoned and executed by the Nazis in 1944.

(3) The Courtyard off Józefińska Street

After visiting *Muzeum Apteka Pod Orłem*, turn left outside onto Targowa Street, then right onto Józefińska Street. Stop on the corner. On the opposite side of Józefińska Street, just past the corner and to the left of a large, white, modern apartment block, is a courtyard where my family and I went to our local prayer house, or *Beit Midrash*, at Limanowskiego Street 13. In the courtyard, below the steep-roofed apartment building with several long balconies, there was a bakery that I went to every Friday, before Sabbath, taking the traditional *challah* bread and cake my mother had made to be baked, since our coal-burning oven was for cooking only, not baking. I also carried the *cholent* my mother prepared. Crumbs from from my mother's baked cakes were the reward for my work! In the courtyard there were several traders including a tinsmith and a carpenter and delivery wagons. Sometimes I would take a chicken on Friday to the kosher slaughterer at the other end of Krakusa Street. All this of course ended after the start of the war.

On my last day in the ghetto, which was liquidated in March 1943, my father, my two brothers, and I were marched along this street to the *Umschlagplatz* with our permitted 25 kilograms of possessions while terror and death reigned around us.

(4) Mikveh

Continue along the sidewalk on the right, up Józefińska Street, stopping at the white modern multi-storey block, Józefińska Street 5. On this site there used to be a *mikveh*, the Jewish ritual bathhouse. I accompanied my father here on Fridays before the Sabbath.

(5) The Central Hospital

Almost opposite, on the corner of Węgierska Street and Józefińska Street is an older building (Józefińska Street 14), now city council offices, which during the time of the ghetto was the Central Hospital;[8] before the existence of the ghetto, the hospital had been on Skawińska Street in Kazimierz.

On the morning of 28 October 1942, all the patients and staff at the Central Hospital were shot.

(6) Arbeitsamt – Work under the Nazis

Next door to the hospital, at Józefińska Street 10, were the *Arbeitsamt* labor offices. Here the German occupying forces kept and maintained records of inhabitants of the ghetto, about where they lived and what compulsory labor they had been assigned.

Compulsory labor for Jews followed a decree on 26 October 1939 made by Governor General Hans Frank (who had taken up offices in the magnificent splendour of Kraków's Wawel Castle): all Jews aged between 16 and 60 were ordered to work. The office operated from March 6 1940 until it was closed down after the ghetto deportation in October 1943.

Everyone in the ghetto had to have a yellow *Kennkarte* personal identity card. With a *Blauschein*, a blue slip, the *Kennkarte* showed that the holder was a legal resident of the ghetto and could leave the ghetto and work. Working meant that you were not usually deported during some of the *Aktionen*, or round-ups.[9]

The only time Jews were sent out other than for work was for what were called 'anthropological examinations': all Jews in the ghetto between the ages of 14 and 25 were sent to the former Geographical Institute on Grodzka Street where they were examined by a doctor who made a report concerning measurements – weight, height, shape of skull.[10] Whether these examinations were just an excuse that German doctors had created for getting out of serving in the war, or whether they really believed in Nazism's theories about the difference between races is anybody's guess.

SS raids occurred even before the ghetto. I can remember several times when German trucks drove up and surrounded people, forcing them at gunpoint into the truck for work. In later raids, people were shot and the bodies could not be removed for a while. Later, some white powder, maybe chlorine, was scattered.

Thousands of workers, including those who continued to address each other as 'Doctor', 'Attorney', or 'Professor', went out of the ghetto in groups each morning under armed guard and returned the same way. Ghetto workers sometimes worked together with Polish laborers. Most of these were from the outskirts of Kraków. Never the upper-class Poles, but only because they had already been murdered.

Curfew in the ghetto was at nine in the evening. Each person was recognizable as a Jew by having to wear on their right sleeve a white band showing a blue Star of David.[11] It was not permitted to take this off: first there was threat of a fine, then jail, and ultimately death. The constant danger of being informed on and consequently being punished ensured that people did not attempt to escape the work group. If anyone did, the rest of the group faced the usual punishment: execution.

'One for all and all for one', was the mocking Nazi version of the Scouts' well-known adage. If one prisoner escaped, ten were murdered.

So, apart from the young, the sick and the old, the ghetto was largely empty during the day. Of course, some people tried to leave, or hide under false papers. Few were successful. Anyway, where could they go? Some tried to join the underground resistance movement. Many came back after hiding for a few days or weeks. Some had even been to Warsaw and stayed for a time in the ghetto there.

2 The 'Final Solution': Mass deportations from the ghetto, June and October 1942

In 1941, the war was heightened with the German advance against the Soviets occupying eastern Poland, destroying the Molotov–Ribbentrop 'non-aggression' agreement. In December, Japan and America had declared war. A month later, in January 1942, at the Wannsee Conference, the decision was made to implement the *Endlösung der Judenfrage*, 'The Final Solution of the Jewish Problem' in Europe, aimed at and resulting in the murder of millions of people.

The first ghetto deportation had already occurred in October 1941. Due to 'overcrowding', around 1,000 ghetto inhabitants were sent to the Lubelskie province in eastern Poland.[12] In the Kraków Ghetto, two large deportation actions took place, from 1 to 8 June and between 27 and 28 October 1942, as part of Operation Reinhardt.

On the night of 3 June, an announcement went out that all documents were to be checked. Anyone who did not have a permit was to be held. During the night, the *Sonderdienst*[13] and *OD* (*Ordnungsdienst* – Jewish Police) searched everyone, in the houses and the hospitals. This went on until the morning of the following day.

At 6 am, an announcement was made that those who were to be deported could take 25 kilograms of possessions. Anyone without specially marked identity cards providing them with permission to stay were evacuated and deported via train. People were ordered to leave their apartments open with the keys in the lock. The panic and confusion that erupted was met by an escalation of violence, resulting in the murder of hundreds of people in Plac Zgody: today Plac Bohaterów Getta – Ghetto Heroes Square. This massacre of innocents became known as Bloody Thursday. People were pushed and beaten with rifle butts. Those who did not follow orders, or were not lucky, were simply shot in the streets. Many hundreds were shot, including Mordechaj Gebirtig, the writer of the well-known songs *Rajzele* and *Es Brent* (*It's Burning*):[14]

Brothers, our poor town is burning;   There may come a time,
Angry winds are blowing,   When all of us shall perish,
And people are fanning the flames,   In these circles of fire –
Or looking on,   As you stand and look on …
Watching with their arms folded,
As our town burns.

One might think that Gebirtig was writing about the ghetto, but in fact he wrote *It's Burning* in 1938, a year before the war, in protest against Polish anti-Semitism. At the same time, these were prophetic words.

Personally, I remember local incidents of pre-war anti-Semitism. Occasionally young people, some my Catholic schoolmates, would shout, 'There's a Jew! Let's get him!' This was sometimes followed by stone-throwing or a chase. I felt I was running for my life as I heard the words, 'Dirty Jew, why don't you go to Palestine!'

We also had to be careful about going by the local Saint Joseph Church (on Rynek Podgórski), especially around a Catholic holiday. Easter, for instance, was the time when priests commonly repeated the hateful libel that Jews were Christ-killers, accused us of preparing Passover matzoh from the blood of innocent Christian children, or some other hateful nonsense.

At times like this, my parents would not let me out of the apartment house. All the same, I remember being spat upon and kicked – then, of course, without understanding why.

It may have been just naive childish hatred. But it was, of course, a product of what these children had learned from somewhere, their parents, their teachers, or their priests.

You see, we were not addressed as Poles. We were addressed as Jews, while they were addressed as Poles. We were always called 'the Jewish nation'. So we were not considered Poles, although my parents' parents' parents were born in this country. And not only I, but all Jews were thought of as Christ-killers.

Because of these experiences, the church and its cross became fearful symbols for me in my child's mind. I didn't even want to look up at it, since it was such a frightening symbol to me.

Once the ghetto wall had been built, the church continued to tower over us – its presence reminding us that whatever else was going on, the undeserved attacks on Jews had grown into a war against our very existence.

Of course, compared with German anti-Semitism, Polish Jew-hatred was a far, far smaller beast. There is a great difference between the two. Although there were discriminatory laws in Poland regarding Jews, the attacks were mostly ignorant verbal taunts. The physical assaults that did occur were carried out by a lawless rabble of young thugs. In Germany, however, the fascist scum had gained charge of the country. They put their anti-Semitic jibes into practice on a vast and unprecedented scale.

All those not called for deportation hid in their homes following the mass shootings. The dead were buried in a mass grave at the Jewish cemetery in Płaszów. The deportation trains headed east, their human cargo packed together in closed cattle cars.

On Saturday, 6 June a second registration process was announced. Everyone in the ghetto was told to bring their *Kennkarte* to a designated building on Józefińska Street. Those Jews who were not to be deported were issued a new *Blauschein*. This process was carried out entirely by the Gestapo. Those who were not issued a card were detained on

7. Ghetto main gate and *Judenrat* building, Limanowskiego Street
(Muzeum Historyczne Miasta Krakowa)

the spot, taken to the former Optima chocolate factory courtyard (11, illus. 4, page 7), and left there without provisions
until they were marched, on the following Monday, to
Prokocim station. There, they were loaded onto trains. A few
individuals were taken to the nearby Julag, an abbreviation
for *Judenlager*, a new labour camp specifically for Jews.[15]

By 8 June, an estimated 6,500 people had been deported
from the ghetto and 130 killed there. Twelve thousand people
remained in the ghetto. In other words, a third of the ghetto
inhabitants had been 'resettled'.[16]

From the June and October deportations, it is estimated that
a total of 11,000[17] Jews from Kraków were sent to the extermination centre at Bełżec in the east of Poland, south of Zamość,
where it is calculated that over 600,000 Jews were murdered.

In the October deportation, *Sonderdienst* and Polish 'Blue
Police' assembled in the evening to greet the returning
workers with the news of a deportation the following day.
Then all the workers had to line up. Those who were judged

fit enough to work were kept, while the rest were deported along with their wives and children.

You may wonder why people didn't escape. Some did. They tried to hide under false papers. But few were successful. After several days or weeks they usually came back to the ghetto. Where else could they go?

After the October deportation, hardly a day went by without further round-ups and shootings. Often the bodies remained in the streets for a while. After they were taken away, white powder was scattered.

Suicides were common. Some people had lost all hope. Whole families poisoned themselves with cyanide.

I was fortunate. I never lost my will to survive.

(7) The Main Gate to the Ghetto

Continue to the end of Józefińska Street and turn left onto Brodzińskiego Street. This was one corner of the ghetto. All the windows and gates you can see were barricaded or bricked in. You are now walking outside of the former ghetto. Carry on along Brodzińskiego Street to the corner, stopping before the streetcar tracks on Rynek Podgórski.

Where Limanowskiego Street and Podgórski market meet was the main gate of the ghetto. There were four ghetto gates. The main gate connected the German police station and *Judenrat* building at Rynek Podgórski 1 with the building at Rynek Podgórski 15. Jews working outside the ghetto left through this gate, and Aryans entering the ghetto received their passes here. Gate II was at Kącik Street. Gate III existed between 31 and 50 Lwowska Street. It was through this gate that people were marched to Płaszów concentration camp. Gate IV was situated on the corner of Limanowskiego Street and Lwowska Street.

Streetcar number 3 went right through the ghetto – beneath the sign, engraved in Yiddish, *Jüdischer Wohnbezirk* (Jewish residential district) – without stopping. And, though we were not permitted to use them, the streetcars kept running through the ghetto for almost the whole time of its existence.

Every day, lots of people rode through the ghetto, looking with curiosity at the conditions under which we had to live.

Ordnungsdienst – The ghetto police

In the beginning of the ghetto period, I was able to jump on and off the back of the streetcar inside the ghetto if the driver was cooperative. Though, often, we were carefully watched.

Within the ghetto, a Jewish police force, the *Ordnungsdienst* (Order Duty) was established by the Nazis to maintain order among ghetto occupants. The *OD* was supposed to be obedient to the SS and the Gestapo. Not all *OD* men were collaborators. There were some who were good, who worked for the *OD* in the small hope that they might be able to save themselves and their families. Others, including the *OD* leader Symche Spira, blindly assisted the SS and Gestapo. Spira is thought to have informed the Nazis about members of the *ŻOB* resistance movement, leading to their deaths. Along with other collaborators and their families, Spira was shot and burned on Chujowa Górka at Płaszów labor camp in late 1943. Other ethnic Polish or Jewish informers, *szmalcownik* or scum, were killed by the Polish Underground with the assistance of the *ŻOB*.

(8) Rynek Podgórski

Cross the streetcar rails to Rynek Podgórski, stopping in the middle of the square in front of the church. In the years before the Nazi invasion, I used to accompany my mother or father to the Rynek – the market – to purchase milk, butter, eggs, cheeses, fresh vegetables, or an occasional chicken. I liked the excitement of lots of people shouting and selling their goods, and the special aroma of the market.

The main building on Rynek Podgórski is the Saint Joseph Church. Although it's a beautiful church, I rarely looked up at the church when I walked by because, as a child, I was afraid. Being a Jew, I was the butt of verbal taunts or was pushed down and spat upon. After all, to many Catholic children, I was a Christ-killer.

A few years ago while telling people my story, I caught myself bending my head to avoid looking up at the church. It was an unconscious action, because I was always afraid when people came out of the church that they would attack me as a Jew.

I was able to get rid of my fear only several years ago, through confronting it – by walking into the church.

It's quite beautiful inside. But this is what happened there.

Julius Madritsch and the Madritsch clothing factory

My mother and Miriam, my sister, worked first for Oskar Schindler's company (the factory was outside the ghetto on Lipowa Street), then for Julius Madritsch. The Madritsch factory was at Rynek Podgórski 3, though the entrance from inside the ghetto was opposite Węgierska Street 10. There they sewed German army uniforms until the day prior to their deportation. On that day, they were simply told not to report to work. 'Unnecessary' workers were being deported. The factory remained in operation even after the liquidation of the ghetto.

Julius Madritsch has been called the Guardian Angel of the ghetto and Płaszów camp because, although he was a Nazi Party member, he tried to help Jews by giving them extra food supplies. He helped over 4,000 people, Jews and non-Jews. Madritsch was eventually arrested in Kraków and sent to Berlin on 3 November 1944, after the Nazis learned that he had been assisting the Polish Underground. Through his contacts he managed to secure his release after only a few days. Madritsch lived after the war in close contact with many of those whose lives he had saved. He was given the title of Righteous Gentile by Yad Vashem in Jerusalem, and Jewish survivors set up the Madritsch Association. Madritsch wrote in his autobiography, *Menschen In Not! (People in Plight)*, about his experiences after the war. He died in June 1984.[18]

Facing the front of the church, go left onto Rękawka

Street, then turn left onto Węgierska Street. At the beginning of this and the next three streets, in the ghetto's early days, was a 14-foot-high (4 metre) brick wall. Shards of glass were embedded on top of the wall to deter escape.

(9) Zuker's Synagogue

Stop at Węgierska Street 5, now an art gallery. This building was Zuker's Synagogue, built between 1879 and 1881. It housed the *Beit Midrash Hasidim* (House of Hassidic Learning). The synagogue was officially closed and taken over by the Nazis in August 1942 by order of the *Generalgouvernement*, which gave it to the Hermes company for use as a warehouse.

It was the only distinctive synagogue building of this sort in my immediate neighbourhood, though there were many other prayer houses or *Stiebl.*

Go back to Rękawka Street and continue left to the next street, Krakusa Street. Continue to where you see the sign for Krakusa Street 9. This is the apartment house where I was born (10 on map).

3 My family home

My family comprised my parents, my two brothers, Solomon and Natek, and my sister Miriam. I was the youngest. We all lived in one room. This was our original residence before the ghetto. During the time of the ghetto, people often had to share houses and apartments. But there were already six of us and our apartment was very small. My father Jacob, who was born in Dąbrowa, near Tarnów, was a shoemaker by trade. There were several shoemakers in my family: my grandfather Shlomo Zalman Zwirn, and Joel Zwirn, my grandmother Ciwie's only son, who lived at 24 Kalwaryjska Street with his wife and daughter. I remember Joel with his pockmarked face. He was a learned man in the Jewish tradition.

Though most of my family lived in Podgórze, some lived in Kazimierz. I remember that one of my grandmother Ciwie's brothers, Jacob Schifer, lived on Floriańska Street, near Rynek Główny. Jacob was an artist and he used to display his works on the street near Wawel Castle. He had two sons and one daughter. My grandmother had another brother named Leibisch Schifer, a farmer in a village near Okocim.

To the left of the apartment gate (now a storefront) lived my grandmother, Ciwie Schifer. She was born in either Brzesko or the nearby village of Okocim; her father's name was Berl.

When I first looked at Krakusa Street on my first return in 1981, the one-room apartment in which the six of us lived seemed smaller. Although it no longer existed, there had been a fourth window that was ours. I remembered the friends I played with and the windows of their homes. Once inside our old apartment, I remembered where the stove had been. Our source of light was a kerosene lamp and we brought water in

8. My family home, 9 Krakusa Street, 2001 (Sakiewicz)

from the courtyard. To the left of our window was a cabinet containing a bottle of Schnapps. My father made the *kiddush* blessing for the Sabbath here when he returned from *shul* or synagogue. The hallway was a pantry for preserves, sacks of potatoes, and other staples.

What my parents did

My parents had a tobacco concession. My father was also a peddler. He travelled or walked carrying a backpack and two suitcases around the greater Kraków area selling billiard-table supplies as well as toothpicks to inns, bars and hotels. One time, I recall, my father sold a billiard table. A deal went wrong somehow so we had the table in our single room, and my brothers slept on it. We were poor. But at that time I never knew it.

ANCESTRAL FAMILY TREE

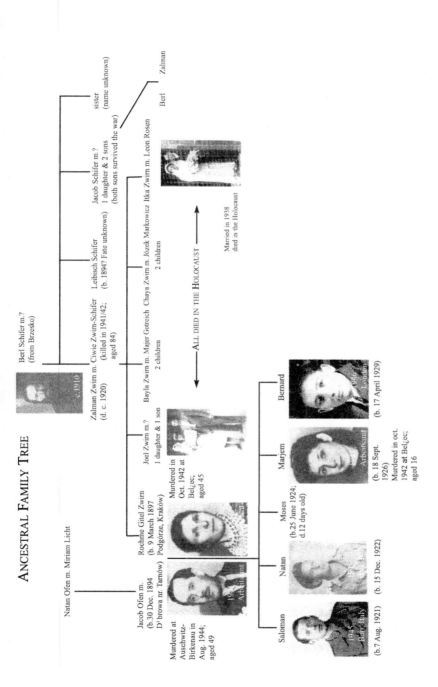

Natan Ofen m. Miriam Licht

Bert Schifer m.?
(from Brzesko)

sister
(name unknown)

Zalman Zwirn m. Ciwie Zwirn-Schifer
(d. c. 1920)   (killed in 1941/42;
                      aged 84)

Leibisch Schifer
(b. 1894? Fate unknown)

Jacob Schifer m.?
1 daughter & 2 sons
(both sons survived the war)

Bert   Zalman

Jacob Ofen m.
(b. 30 Dec. 1894
D'browa nr Tarnów)

Rochme Gitel Zwirn
(b. 9 March 1897
Podgórze, Kraków)

Joel Zwirn m.?
1 daughter & 1 son

Bayla Zwirn m. Majer Gotreich Chaya Zwirn m. Józek Markowicz Itka Zwirn m. Leon Rosen
2 children   2 children

Murdered at
Auschwitz-
Birkenau in
Aug. 1944;
aged 49

Murdered in
Oct. 1942 at
Bełżec;
aged 45

← ALL DIED IN THE HOLOCAUST →

Married in 1938
died in the Holocaust

Saloman

Natan

Moses

Marjem

Bernard

(b. 7 Aug. 1921)

(b. 15 Dec. 1922)

(b.25 June 1924;
d.12 days old)

(b. 18 Sept.
1926)
Murdered in oct.
1942 at Bełżec;
aged 16

(b. 17 April 1929)

9. Ancestral family tree (Jacobs/Sitek)

I think we had a very rich life. We didn't have many things, but grandmother was next door and my uncle lived down the street. We helped each other. And we had other relatives all over the city.

We also sold cigarettes, matches and newspapers from our apartment window facing the street. People would knock on the window to buy a single cigarette, or sometimes a whole pack! Since my father was also a shoemaker, people would come to give my father their shoes to repair. During the ghetto period, father made boots for the German army in the former Optima chocolate factory on Krakusa, behind our courtyard.

There were searches as he came out of the shoe factory with the other workers, to make sure that useful tools and supplies were not stolen. For shoe repairs, my father had to get leather. To bring the leather home, my father nailed four pieces, soles and heels, to his own shoes. He walked home with the new leather on his old shoes. At home he took the pieces off and used them to repair other people's shoes which, during the war, he sometimes gave to me to trade for food on my smuggling trips outside of the ghetto.

In those days, when a Jewish man wanted to get married, one of two things were required of him: either he had to have money or he had to have a trade. No money and no trade meant no girl. There was no talking of living on love. It didn't exist back then.

So my father apprenticed with my grandfather who lived next door. When his apprenticeship finished, he was allowed to marry my mother. They were married in 1920. The wedding took place in my grandmother's two rooms. The photo still exists.

The honor and integrity of the Austrian army
During the First World War, my father was in the Austro-Hungarian army. Most of south-western Poland, including Kraków, was then under the rule of the Austrian Empire. It was only at the end of the war in 1918 that Poland regained its independence. A few years later, my father was in Marshal

Józef Piłsudski's legions in their battles with the Ukrainians. Just over twenty years later, of course, the Austrian army returned under Hitler's swastika to begin its savagery across Europe.

Austria had a long history of anti-Semitism. While not as brutal as the Russian tsar's occupation of eastern Poland, with constant pogroms, the Austrian authorities practised clear anti-Semitism.[19] One way they discriminated against Jews concerned Jewish marriages. Orthodox Jewish couples, since they were married by rabbis, did not go to the local city magistrate to obtain a civil marriage contract. The Austrian authorities, however, ruled that these marriages were invalid, and in the eyes of the law were illegal. As a result, the children of these marriages were considered illegitimate. This included my parents, whose own parents were married, of course, under Jewish law. When Poland gained independence in 1919, this practice was slowly but finally abolished.

Our courtyard

At the back of our apartment there is a courtyard that you can enter or, if it's locked, see through a newly-added steel gate to the right of the storefront door. Where the door is now, there were old apartment windows until just a few years ago. It was the place where we built our temporary *succah* hut and marked *Rosh Chodesh*, greeting the new moon at the beginning of every month. The balconies were then completely glassed-in to keep out the winter snow and rain. The courtyard was also the playground for me and my friends. I spent many hours playing in this courtyard. I remember games of hide-and-seek and the inviting smell of noodle soup with beans. It was a great place for hide-and-seek. So many places to hide. Little did I know that these games would turn into a life-saving device.

Our neighbors on Krakusa Street

I remember the people and friends that I used to play with, those who lived next to us in the same building, and what they did. On the ground floor were Wachtel, umbrella sales and repairs; Błoński the butcher; Goldsztof's grocery store; Spingarn, an old maid; and Tzanger the beggar. Then, on the first floor, lived the Goldsztofs – five people including my friend Hamek, the youngest of the siblings, whose mother made what I remember was the best bean soup! There was also Lerhaft, the apartment owner, who was somehow related to a cousin of mine. Then there was the Katz family of five and, next to them, the Hofsteter family, also five: parents and three daughters. And then there was Kenerowa, and Wicek, her son, who was the best friend of my brother Sam. Finally, on the second and top floors, there was the Bernhut family, comprising Salwina and four boys. I remember three of them: Józek, Salek and the oldest Moniek. Their father owned a *doroszka*, a horse carriage, in which he took us for rides on his way to the horse stable.

I met Józek in Los Angeles about fifteen years ago, the only survivor of the Holocaust from his family.

Apart from Józek, my brothers and me, all of them disappeared – there's no one else surviving that I knew from before the war.

All these people were Jews. The only Catholic was Michałowa, the caretaker. I don't know what happened to her, but I never saw her again ...

(11) The Optima Chocolate Factory

The large Optima building, visible immediately behind the courtyard gate, used to be a chocolate factory. If you can imagine, the whole building's aroma was of chocolate, and the surrounding buildings, too. And, so, because of that, I am addicted to chocolate – I'm a 'chocaholic'.

I had many adventures before the war begging for chocolate, with the help of my friends who had to watch out for a potentially mean watchman. It was here that I learned about cooperation. I used to jump over the wall there and beg for a piece of chocolate from the workers. In order to do that I had to arrange things with my friends: they would go up to the highest window inside our building, facing the courtyard, and from there could watch for the factory caretaker who had a dog. When I jumped down, they warned me whether he was coming. If I got a piece of chocolate I used to have to share it with them. They were my partners. No cooperation with my friends, no chocolate.

The chocolate factory was shut down soon after the occupation. Instead, some Jewish craftsmen – fur-makers, tailors and shoemakers (including my father) – worked for the company *Zentrale für Handwerkslieferungen* located in the factory. The Optima building yard was also a centre for gathering people destined for deportation or, as was said in the ghetto, the *Himmelfahrt* – the trip to heaven.

4 My cousin Ignac, my grand-mother, and life in the ghetto

When the war began, on the first day that the Germans marched into Kraków in September 1939, I was not yet 11 years old. My cousin Ignac came to see my parents on the first day of the war. He was dressed in a Polish army uniform. But what I really remember was that he had two left boots. Was this supposed to be a joke? I do not know. During the war, he fought in General Anders' army. My brothers met him in Bari, in Italy, while they were in the Polish army. Ignac survived the war and I saw him next in London.

The day the German army entered Kraków, there was a curfew declared and everyone was supposed to stay inside with the windows closed, but I wandered out of the apartment house and went to the corner of Krakusa Street and Limanowskiego Street. I was young. It was all exciting, and I was curious.

So, on hearing the sound of vehicles, I went out to see the arriving German soldiers. One of them jumped down from a truck and shot in my direction with a rifle, hitting a nearby wall. I think he just wanted to frighten me, because he was very close. German soldiers were well trained. And I was just a little kid. Anyway, I ran away – and he was satisfied.

During this time and even before the ghetto, the area was surrounded many times. The Germans used to come and surround a whole block. And everyone in the apartment houses had to get out into the street.

They started picking up children and older people. Since I was the youngest, my father and my mother told me where to go and hide. I was under age for legal work and so was in extra danger. I hid in basements or in roof-spaces and waited until

10. A round-up of Jews in the Podgórski market, 5 and 6 December 1941 (Fundacja Shalom)

someone from my family called me after the raids were over. They said, 'Don't come out until we tell you to come out and you recognize our voice!' I heard screams and shooting and all that. But I had to keep quiet, until one of my parents or my sister came and told me I could come out – '*It's all over.*'

While everyone else in my family was forced to work, I had to hide. I always had to hide since the young and old were being rounded-up. Work permits were only for those aged between 14 and 60. The young, the old and the sick were targets of these raids, rounded up since they were considered by the Nazi mentality as worthless mouths to feed, only because they did not work.

I remember, in the years before the war, my mother making a tapestry using a frame. She worked so hard at it that it affected her eyes. It was full of colour, showing the infant Moses hiding from the Egyptians amongst the bulrushes. Like Moses, I too had to hide only because I was Jewish.

It was after one of the times I hid under the roof that, when I came back down, my grandmother was gone, taken at gunpoint. My grandmother Ciwie Zwirn-Schifer, 84 years old, disappeared from my life. I never saw or heard from her again.

One of her cousins was said to have lived to be 104 years old. Fortunately, his eyes were not fated to see the destruction that was to come, since he passed away a few months before the start of the war.

It was not only my grandmother. My uncles and other people started to disappear too. My whole family started to disappear in this fashion. Eventually, they almost all 'disappeared'. If I had not hidden, I would have gone too.

When I think of it now, it was amazing that I survived the ghetto.

5 'Resettlement'

The early deportations were deceptive. 'Resettlement' (*Aussiedlung*) was the term usually given. People were being helped onto the trains. Families were separated, but those who went took what they could, looking forward to a new life when they might next see their husbands and sons. They did not know what awaited them at the end of the train ride. While this happened, photographers took pictures to show to the world the humaneness of the Germans in their treatment of residents from the Jewish Quarter who had to be resettled due to 'overcrowding'. The Germans also took photos of men they hanged to use as material to say that Polish Jews were murdering their fellow Poles: Propaganda.

In the ghetto, we started to hear that deported people had been taken to some place and, later on, other people got letters saying that things were hard but OK. That was the general message: we are well, we have food and drink. But many of these people were dead by the time we received the mail they had been forced to write. This was just another one of the many strategies adopted by the Nazis to deceive their victims and their victims' families.

Although we now know what took place, mass murder was not yet conceivable to those of us who lived in the ghetto. We had difficulty in understanding the barbarism of the guards, and it was beyond all understanding that the leaders of a supposedly highly educated and civilized nation could allow such things to happen.

Forty years later, as I traveled by train through Poland, I wondered if the cattle cars I saw were the same ones used to transport my mother and sister to Bełżec, the death camp near Zamość.

(12) The Jewish Orphanage

Cross to the other side of the street to Krakusa Street 8 where there is a wall plaque: *Dom Sierot 1936*. This marks the former site of a Jewish orphanage that existed before the ghetto. After the June 1943 deportations, the orphanage was moved to Józefińska Street 31. It was liquidated following the October deportation the same year. About 300 children were put onto trains and deported with their guardians, Dawid Kurzmann and Mr and Mrs Feurstin. All children in the 'B' area of the ghetto were murdered at the time of the ghetto liquidation on 14 March 1943. There was another orphanage on Józefińska Street 12.

Go through the gate and you will see another wall-plaque inside the entrance in both Polish and Hebrew lettering.

My Aunts and Uncles

Continue walking to the corner of Krakusa Street and Limanowskiego Street. On the left-hand side corner is an apartment building painted yellow. Behind the second floor balcony, at the corner of the street, lived my aunt Chaya Zwirn-Schifer with her two children – both had distinct red hair – and her husband Józek Markowicz. The lower balcony was theirs.

I never saw them again shortly after the creation of the ghetto.

(13)   Our move to Limanowskiego Street 5 – reduction of the ghetto, June 1942

A week after the June 1942 deportations, the ghetto was reduced by putting up a barbed-wire fence along Limanowskiego Street. Parts of the ghetto wall were knocked down; some of Krakusa and Węgierska streets, all of Rękawka and Czarnieckiego, and the right side of Limanowskiego Street were all separated from the new area of the ghetto. The ghetto was now made up of just five streets. Divided into several blocks, ghetto inhabitants from different blocks worked on different days of the week.[20]

My immediate family and I had to move to Limanowskiego Street 5, the apartment where my youngest aunt lived, Aunt Itka Zwirn-Schifer. She married her husband, a furrier named Leon Rosen, just before the war. I can remember their wedding celebration in my grandmother's apartment, next door to my family's home on Krakusa Street.

To see where we lived, turn left on Limanowskiego Street and go one block to the corner of Węgierska Street. Number 5 is opposite. Cross the street.

A new wooden ghetto gate was built next to the building where we lived, beside the adjacent barbed-wire fence in front of our house on the sidewalk.

6 My mother and Miriam disappear, while my brother Nathan helps wounded Germans, 27–28 October 1942

My father and I worked in our apartment repairing shoes with wooden nails. My older brothers, Nathan and Salomon, did not live there with us. My brothers were rounded up several times. They disappeared and then, thankfully, reappeared.

I would go out to smuggle food into the ghetto. I remember smuggling food to a starving family. There were secret places where you could get over the ghetto wall, especially during the early days of the ghetto. When the ghetto was cut in half, my father and mother and sister, sometimes my brothers, used to come, look out for the police, and lift up the barbed wire. Then they said, 'OK now! Go!' I slipped under and headed very fast into the Podgórze hills nearby. There, I traded things for food. I did that many times.

My mother, Rochme Gitel-Schifer, and my sister Miriam disappeared from our new apartment while I was out of the ghetto, smuggling food. One day, in October 1942, I was sent out by my parents earlier than usual. Now, when I think back, it is clear that they were expecting something and wanted me to be away, just in case, for my own safety.

When I tried to get back into the ghetto, I could not because the whole ghetto was surrounded by extra troops of SS and Polish police. And there were the *Ordnungsdienst* Jewish police inside the ghetto. I heard shootings and screams. I could not get back in. So I waited until it was all over, hiding not too far from where I later slipped back into the ghetto. This was the fourth large *Aktion*. In charge of the entire *Aktion* and transport was Gestapo *Obersturmbannführer* Wilhelm Haase.[21]

The night before, the Germans had made my brother Nathan help them at a nearby railroad station. They were bringing back their wounded and frozen soldiers from the Russian front. Jews from the ghetto were ordered to carry them across the railroad tracks to an *Entlausung* (delousing) train, where they received medical attention. They moaned and groaned with pain. One young German SS man called Nathan over in broken Polish. He called him 'friend'. He wanted Nathan to help him. This made my brother very angry, but, all the same, he carried him on his back. The SS man screamed with pain, but no one paid any special attention to this man since there were other soldiers crying out at the same time. For a moment, Nathan felt good in seeing their pain but soon afterwards felt terrible, thinking of himself as having stooped to their level. In the morning, Nathan and the other men returned under guard to the ghetto.

As he reached the bridge over the river, Nathan saw a large number of trucks heading into the ghetto. As he went through the ghetto gate into Plac Zgody, he noticed more trucks and SS men assembled there. As Nathan walked to Józefińska Street, he saw men, women and children being guarded by the SS and moved to the square. There, while I was out of the ghetto, he saw our mother and Miriam, our sister. Nathan tried to reach them but he was stopped by an SS man who hit him with his rifle butt on both sides of Nathan's face. He began to bleed. My mother saw Nathan and motioned to him to run. He saw little Miriam holding on to our mother's skirt looking petrified. This was the last time Nathan saw them.

My mother and sister were gone. Sam and Nathan were rounded up several times, disappearing but then reappearing. But my mother and Miriam never came back. My father was never the same again. His wife and daughter had gone forever – taken away at gunpoint. I remember returning to the ghetto and seeing my father with his face in his hands.

They had been taken to the extermination camp at Bełżec.[22]

The Liquidation of the Central Hospital

On the morning of 28 October 1942, at the same time that my mother and sister were rounded up for deportation, patients and staff at the Central Hospital on Józefińska Street were being murdered. The Nazis went in and started just shooting anybody on the spot. Killing, killing and killing.

Afterwards, my brother Nathan and others had the task of throwing the bodies out of the windows into the courtyard. There were little babies in the hospital. Some were just a few days old and still crying. Nathan saw German SS men pick up babies by their feet and throw them through the window. Outside, they were hitting them against the sidewalk again and again, until there was silence. They were doing this with all the little babies.

My brother and the others had to pick up the corpses and load them onto trucks and horse-drawn wagons that they then walked alongside to Płaszów, guarded by Ukrainian men in SS uniforms.[23]

At Płaszów, hundreds of people were thrown into the mass graves there, some of them not yet dead.

On one of the last transports of corpses, of which there were a number, the SS started shooting at the people in the commando working on moving the bodies, since they wanted to wipe out all witnesses of their crime. My brother, seeing what was happening, jumped into the pit. Covered in blood, and acting as if dead himself, Nathan stayed in the mound of bodies to avoid being spotted. Anyone who moved was shot straight in the head by the couple of men who stayed around looking for any possible escapees.

Nathan survived that night. After everything had calmed down, he crawled out from under a heap of bodies, under the cover of night.

(14) Our Neighborhood Synagogue

Turn around and go back along the Limanowskiego sidewalk, passing Krakusa Street. On the corner on Limanowskiego Street 13 is where our neighborhood synagogue was located. Now it is an art gallery.

(15) Hospital for Chronic Diseases

At Limanowskiego Street 15 was the *Szpital dla Przewlekle Chorych* – Hospital for Chronic Diseases. Some people were hidden here during the June deportation. After the October deportation, the SS came here and murdered all of the people who had difficulties walking. Dr Jakub Kranz, head of the hospital, died with his patients.

(16) The Cheder – My Jewish school

Continue on, and cross the street, stopping at the corner of Czarnieckiego Street, the second street on the right.

This is the route I regularly followed to the *Cheder* (Jewish school) at the Talmud Torah, the red brick building on Rękawka Street 30 at the far end of Czarnieckiego Street. I remember going to the *Cheder* for Yiddish lessons. When *Cheder* was over, we often had to run from Polish boys throwing stones or chasing us with sticks.

11. Plaque on remaining part of the ghetto wall, Lwowska Street (Sakiewicz)

The Nazi authorities closed the *Cheder*. All Jewish schools were closed on 5 May 1940. Similarly, Polish secondary schools and universities were closed. Non-Jewish primary schoolchildren, who learned only German language and arithmetic, were made to march and raise their arms in salute to the Führer, like the German Hitler Youth. Both the Polish- and Yiddish-language press were liquidated, as were Polish signboards and markers. They were replaced with German ones.

Toward the end of 1939, the *Cheder* became *Żydowski Szpital Zakaźny*, the Jewish Hospital for Infectious Diseases. Dr Aleksander Bieberstein, its director, helped people by hiding them for a while in the hospital. He realized that the Germans would seldom enter the hospital for fear of catching a potentially life-threatening disease.

Following the June 1942 deportations, the hospital was transferred to Plac Zgody 3. When the ghetto was liquidated less than a year later, the patients were shot on a nearby street while the hospital staff, including Dr Bieberstein, were moved to the Płaszów camp. Dr Bieberstein survived the war and went on to become director of social security in Kraków until he left Poland for Israel in 1959.

(17)   Remains of the ghetto wall – Lwowska Street

Continue along Limanowskiego Street to the second set of traffic lights and cross the streetcar tracks to rejoin Józefińska Street. Continue along Józefińska Street about 200 feet [75 metres] until the street turns into Lwowska Street. There, on the right, you will see one part of the ghetto wall and an information plaque: 'Here many lived, suffered and perished in the hands of Hitler's perpetrators. From this place they made their last journey.'

You are now outside of what was the ghetto. We, my family and thousands of other people, marched past this wall on our way to Płaszów labor camp during the last days of the ghetto's existence.

7 The end of the ghetto: The start of the Płaszów camp, November 1942

Since November 1942, some of the workers from the ghetto had begun to work on the new camp at Płaszów. Stories about new provisions and better conditions than in the ghetto were circulated. Dawid Guter, president of the *Judenrat*, tried to explain that the camp was intended only for Poles or Jews from France and Hungary. Most knew that the stories were lies meant to prevent alarming people. Since the new camp was being built on the site of a Jewish cemetery, which the Nazis had ordered to be destroyed to make way for the camp, it did not offer much optimism. At the time, however, I hardly knew any of the details.[24] I did what my father told me and kept hoping that things would get better.

In the same month, *Kennkarten* were invalidated, replaced by *Judenkarten*. The ghetto was reduced again. It was on 14 November 1942 that the occupation authorities announced that five principal ghettos were being used to accommodate Jews: Warsaw, Kraków, Lwów, Bełżec (an extermination camp in reality) and Radom. The rest of Poland was declared *Judenrein* – free of Jews.[25]

Second reduction of the ghetto – December 1942
In December 1942, another reduction of the ghetto took place. This time, the ghetto was divided into two sections. In section A lived those fit enough to work; in section B, the old, the sick, and all children under the age of 14.

Kinderheim – *January 1943*

At the start of 1943, the Germans created a *Kinderheim* (children's home), at Józefińska Street 31, in the new Ghetto Section B. Six hundred children came here.[26] The Nazis told everyone that children under the age of 14 would be supervised and cared for in the new home while their parents went to work. Children would be taught how to weave baskets and sew, to help their parents when they were grown up. Soon the ghetto would move to the camp in Płaszów. It was said that the new camp would have shops and better centres for the residents of the ghetto. This was the story the Nazis told those who cared to listen. Few believed them. We were trapped so we had no choice but to listen to what was said and to keep our wits. Those who believed them were the ones who remained optimistic. I stayed hidden. I had to be more careful than ever before.

The liquidation of the Kraków Ghetto, 13 March 1943

The liquidation of the ghetto took place in two stages: an estimated 4,000 working people from Ghetto Section A were deported to Płaszów labor camp on 13 March 1943, while 2,000 to 3,000 were sent to the Auschwitz-Birkenau extermination camp. The next day, the remaining occupants of the ghetto – the old, the sick and the children, all those in Section B – were either taken to Birkenau or shot in the ghetto. Once more, those unable to work were regarded as useless by the efficient Nazis.

It is estimated that 3,000 people were transported from Ghetto Section B and 1,500 people were shot in the ghetto following its liquidation.[27] Children from the *Kinderheim* were shot on Plac Zgody, which means Agreement or Concord Square, the name it was given following the end of the glorious First World War. What an irony!

On the morning of 13 March, SS-*Oberscharführer* Albert Huyar arrived and shot infants, mothers, doctors and nurses at the main hospital on Józefińska in the second large *Aktion* there. My father, brothers and I remained in the square for a large part of the day, while shooting and terror surrounded

12. Liquidation of the ghetto, March 1943 (Muzeum Historyczne Miasta Krakowa)

13. Liquidation of the ghetto, March 1943 (Muzeum Historyczne Miasta Krakowa)

us, later to be marched to the Płaszów slave-labor camp, carrying some clothing, food and cooking pots, as hundreds of others were being shot in the streets.

It is estimated that the deaths of around 3,000 people resulted from the liquidation of the Kraków Ghetto. Perhaps more.

Now the ghetto was really *Judenrein*. The 800-year-old community of Kraków Jews had been irreparably destroyed, its people and the property and artefacts of its culture. Synagogues, Torahs and other holy books were all burned or simply stolen and re-utilized, part of the Nazi's depraved actions.

On 14 March the ghetto in Kraków ceased to exist.

(18) Additional remains of the ghetto wall – Limanowskiego Street

Continue on the sidewalk, turning right at the corner, and cross back over the streetcar tracks to the other side of Limanowskiego Street where the pedestrian crossing is. Ghetto gate IV was located here. Turn left after the crossing and continue on the right-hand side of the street past the corner, proceeding to the far end of the primary school building at Limanowskiego Street 28.

During the war, this building was used by the German command.

Turn right at the end of the school building and go through the steel gate. Approximately one hundred feet (30 metres) further on is the only other remaining section of the old ghetto wall. Although there is no sign marking it, this is the outside of the ghetto wall. It is very low now and has recently been restored. The design remains the same: the top of the wall is in the shape of old Jewish cemetery headstones. Somehow the Germans thought this was a funny touch, knowing the destiny they had chosen for us.

It remains here since it serves as a useful boundary wall for the school, next to it a children's play area.

This is the end of the Ghetto walk.

14. Remaining part of the ghetto wall, off Limanowskiego Street (Sakiewicz)

The Kraków Ghetto Song – by Heniek Grunwald

Chociaż Żydzi mówią veto,
mimo wszystko będzie getto.
Tu w Podgórzu. Wszyscy będą tu!
A kto z nas bdzie uparty,
będzie mieszkał bez kenkarty,
bo któż mu będzie zabronić mógł?

Refrain:
Żydowska dzielnica żydowska policja będzie,

kto coś ukradnie, w żydowskim areszcie
siędzie;
żyd dozorca i żyd lekarz,

żyd kominiarz i żyd aptekarz;

o żydowskie 'cures' będą tu!

O te 'cures,' te kenkarty!
To są autentyczne fakty!
To jest getto –
krakowskie getto tu!

Refrain:
Żydowska dzielnica żydowska policja będzie,

kto coś ukradnie, w żydowskim areszcie
siędzie;
żyd dozorca i żyd lekarz,

żyd kominiarz i żyd aptekarz;

o żydowskie 'cures' będą tu!

Even though the Jews say 'veto,'
there still will be a ghetto, here in Podgórze.
Everybody will be here!
And should someone still object,
no *Kennkarte* will he have,
for who can forbid him to live this way?

There'll be a Jewish district with a Jewish
police,
and there'll be a Jewish jail for anyone
who steals;
there'll be a Jewish chimney-sweep and a
Jewish doctor,
there'll be a Jewish pharmacist and a
Jewish porter.
Oh, and we'll have Jewish *Tzuris* here!

O such *Tzuris*, such *Kennkarten*!
This is how it is, the simple truth!
That's the ghetto –
the Kraków Ghetto here!

There'll be a Jewish district with a Jewish
police,
and there'll be a Jewish jail for anyone
who steals;
there'll be a Jewish chimney-sweep and a
Jewish doctor,
there'll be a Jewish pharmacist and a
Jewish porter.
Oh, and we'll have Jewish *Tzuris* here!

[*Tzuris* is a Yiddish term for problems]
Translated by Katarzyna Jakubiak

PART II

Płaszów Concentration Camp and Julag Labor Camp, 1943–44

8 The walk to Płaszów, March 1943

After our evacuation and deportation from Plac Bohaterów Getta (Ghetto Heroes Square) in March 1943, my father, two brothers and I were marched along Lwowska Street and out the gate onto Wielicka Street, to the labor camp at Płaszów. The camp was located less than two kilometres from the city, in an easterly direction, toward the Wieliczka salt mine.

Following our march to Płaszów, the Nazis rounded-up all the people who were found still hiding in the ghetto, and many from ghetto B, and brought them to the camp, where a deep pit had been dug. More than 2,000 people were killed there in the days following 13 March 1943. A latrine (20 on *Lageplan Konzentrationslager Krakau-Plaszow*, illus. 16, page 53[28]) was built atop the mass grave on the site of the desecrated new Jewish cemetery of Kraków. Next to it stood the quarantine barracks (18 and 19), the clothing warehouse (48), the bathhouse (49), and the station for delousing (50).

To prepare the area for barracks and other buildings, a *bager* digging machine was used. The soil and decomposed bodies wrapped in rotting prayer shawls were removed in this way. 'Going under the tractor' was part of everyday camp jargon.

Remains of bodies were moved in metal wheelbarrows to the hill Chujowa Górka (206) and burned there.[29] As the camp grew in size, this site was used to place extra barracks, and then the ditch Lipowy Dołek (207) was used for the regular mass executions. Teams of prisoners – the so-called *Todenkommando* – were given hammers and made to remove gold teeth from every skull that came out of the earth. This is why the *bager* was known by prisoners as 'The Dentist'.

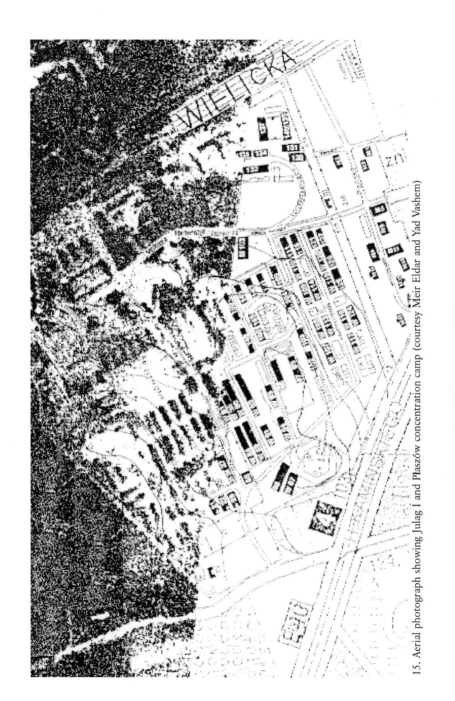

15. Aerial photograph showing Julag I and Płaszów concentration camp (courtesy Meir Eldar and Yad Vashem)

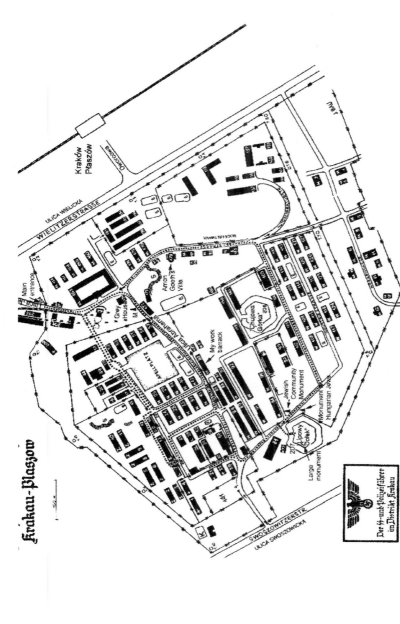

16. Map of Plaszów concentration camp, 1943 (Jacobs/Sitek, from original by Joseph Bau)

The Wieliczka sub-camp

In the middle of 1943, Płaszów was used as a sub-camp for Majdanek, the camp near Lublin.[30] Later, from 10 January 1944, following a visit by dignitaries from Berlin, the camp was transformed from a labor camp into a concentration camp.

Apart from the three Julags, Płaszów had sub-camps in nearby Mielec and Wieliczka. Prisoners, including my brothers Sam and Nathan, were made to work in the Wieliczka salt mines.[31] Sam and Nathan were sent from Płaszów to the Wieliczka camp in spring 1944. There they had *KL* (*Konzentrationslager*) tattooed on their left wrists. After the war, Nathan somehow managed to squeeze the tattoo out. Before then, Nathan had worked at the Bonarka brick kiln during both the ghetto and Płaszów periods. They were sent back to Płaszów in August 1944 when the Wieliczka camp was shut, shortly before the liquidation of Płaszów. Before the evacuation of the Wieliczka camp, four boys hid themselves in the Wieliczka mine. Since the Russian front's advance bombardments could be heard, Sam and Nathan decided it was worth trying to run and join the four boys. So they got ready for their escape, preparing some food for the hiding place. The chance never came, however, and the four boys were tracked down by dogs and sent to Płaszów where they were hanged. One of the boys, Zenek Fuchs, had been Sam's friend.[32]

Most of the prisoners were men, required for work in the stone quarry. Others worked at Płaszów's Kabel factory, and women were taken to work, mostly domestic duties, at the nearby Rakowice airfield. There were also some women prisoners who worked for Madritsch's company making uniforms for the German army. They were placed in an area separated from the male prisoners, but it made no difference. The living conditions were terrible. People were squashed together on *pritschen*, or bunk beds, several to one blanket. The crowding and stench of human bodies was oppressive. But it was a way of sharing body warmth in winter. If we were lucky, we had a blanket. Many people died during the long nights. SS troops, Latvian and Ukrainian guards and the Jewish Orderly

Service were the camp staff. The *Wachmänner* was made up of Russian prisoners who cooperated with the Nazis.[33] Because of their mass extermination work, SS troops were ensured of the privilege of not having to serve on the front line with the ordinary *Wehrmacht*.[34] This honor no doubt motivated them to follow their work methodically. It is probably also the reason why they did not kill all the prisoners at once.

The Chemiker Kommando

From 10 June 1944, there existed in Płaszów a *Chemiker Kommando*, eventually comprising nine Jewish prisoners who professed to have some training and experience in mathematics and scientific engineering. The *Kommando* was ostensibly employed to design a form of gas that would render useless enemy tanks and planes, a fantastic plan conceived by the *Kommando*'s executive of German professors. The prisoners were in fact provided with simple 'high school' tasks. The reason why was never explained to them. It is speculated that the professors had created the *Kommando* in order to keep themselves employed, away from having to fight at the front. Maybe, they also felt that they could assist Jews, whose lives were indeed aided by the existence of the *Kommando*.[35]

Stary Cmentarz Podgórski – the old Catholic cemetery where I hid

If you choose to walk to the site of Płaszów concentration camp, you can visit the old Catholic cemetery on the hill, on the right-hand side just beyond a small monument, before the main crossroads junction of Wielicka Street and al. Powstańców Wielkopolskich. It was here that I hid for a few nights, after having escaped from the Płaszów camp.

Directions to the site of the Płaszów camp

Continue along Wielicka Street, passing under a railroad bridge and past a gas station. You must then go past the steps on your right of the new Catholic cemetery. Continue on the right, past the building-materials supplier at Wielicka Street

57 to walk alongside a metal fence on your right until you come to a corner where there's a business sign that says: Pastan-Pol, ul. Wielicka 61. Bear right here. This is Jerozolimska Street, the way to the destroyed Jewish cemeteries and the former Płaszów Concentration Camp.

The site of the former camp is two tram stops from the area where the ghetto was.

9 My escape from the Płaszów camp and meeting my uncle Majer, Spring 1943

Within three or four days after we were marched to Płaszów, I was ordered to report with other children to the *Appelplatz*. Children were not meant to go to Płaszów. This was why the *Kinderheim* had been created. Some of us, however, had stayed in hiding. During the liquidation of the ghetto and the march to Płaszów, guards watched to make sure that no child left the ghetto – although some who looked old enough to be adults, including me, had managed to join the march. Now, I was loaded with many other children on three *furmanki* (horse-drawn wagons). And it was after we left this camp that I escaped. We were taken out of the camp and started going in the direction of the ghetto. There had been rumors of a mass killing of children. On the wagon, I overheard one of the guards, either a Ukrainian or a Latvian, say that we are going to be shot at some place. Whether this was true, I do not know. Maybe it was to scare us. Or it could even have been to warn us.

Along with several other children, I jumped off the wagon. There was shooting. I just kept going. I did not see what happened to the others. I escaped and hid myself. In the evening, when it was dark, I made my way to the old Catholic cemetery nearby. Near there, houses were being demolished and a bridge was being built. I knew in the ghetto that my uncle Majer Gotreich, the husband of my mother's sister, Bayla Zwirn-Schifer, was working at this construction site as a tanner.

So I hid myself in a building being demolished, under some boards, leaving just enough opening to see out.

In the morning, when I heard movement, I looked out from underneath the boards and saw some forced laborers working nearby. I saw that they were Jewish prisoners. I got someone's attention. I told him, in Yiddish, who I was and who I was looking for. Through speaking with him, while remaining hidden, I managed to make contact with my uncle Majer.

His group had marched from Julag. Majer was working in the group dismantling buildings on Wielicka Street. After a few words he recognized me.

When my uncle came, he pretended to work while he was talking to me. I asked him, 'What can I do? Where can I go?' At that time I was almost 14. My uncle said, 'I don't know where you can go. I don't know of any help for you.' I spoke with him some more and eventually he said I should return with him to the camp. 'They are not shooting many people', he said, 'and you could come back with me. Come back with us'.

I told him no. I would try to make contact with the Cieślik family we knew.

The Cieślik family
I remained at the construction site. Then, when it was dark, I went through the Podgórze hills and came out on Legionów Street, close to the Cieślik's house at 14 Kalwaryjska Street. I went to them because they were friends of my brother Sam. They used to play cards together. It was my only hope of help.

They were not Jews who had all been rounded up, but Catholics.[36] They were the only family I knew that was not Jewish. I remember one time when their daughter had handed me bread through the ghetto's barbed-wire fence. It was only once, but it made a great difference. Our starvation continued, but, because of instances like this one, so did our hope.

The Cieśliks recognized me and took me in right away. Their apartment house was across from where the Hotel Korona now stands but which was used then by the SS. They gave me food and a place to sleep. The next day they told me they would feed me but I had to go that night. They had three children so, since it was punishable by death to shelter Jews, it was too dangerous for me to stay any longer. A normal life did not exist for people on either side of the barbed wire.

I left after dark and walked back through the Podgórze hills, to sleep in the old Catholic cemetery again.

The following day, I made contact again with my uncle in the same way as before. This time I would go with him to Julag. It was the best offer I had, taking a few days to arrange.

I was smuggled into Julag I, which always sounds crazy to people the first time I tell them what happened to me. But there was simply no other place to go at the time. There was no other help for me. What I did was this: I joined a gang of workers on their march back to the labor camp. Walking five abreast, they lifted me up at the camp gate and held me at shoulder height. Somehow, I guess, they knew that the guards were counting feet, not heads. Maybe they had had enough of gazing into our suffering faces.

10 Julag Camp I, Spring–Fall 1943

Once in Julag, I was an unknown, an 'illegal' prisoner. I had to hide in the roof-space for the first two weeks, when everyone else went to work during the day. During the time I was in Julag I had typhus, which is transmitted by lice. Lots of people had it in the camp. I don't know how I lived through that episode. Anyone who was sick had to report to the sickbay. And what the guards were usually doing was taking them to the back of the barracks and shooting them. This is why my uncle told me not to report to the sick-barrack but, once more, to hide under the roof. 'You are going up on the rafters when we go to work and staying there until I come back.' At night I came down and slept with my uncle in the same bunk. So even with the typhoid fever I still had to go up to the rafters for the day. From there I saw Ukrainian guards, who had a different black uniform from the German guards. Through the window below I could see them shooting people. Curled up, I was watching them execute people. Individuals mostly. Sometimes there were two at a time. But, all told, they executed hundreds of people there.

Somehow my uncle managed to get some medicine for me. When I was well again, I was given the registration number of someone who had been killed. This way, I became a 'legal' prisoner.

The camp, although run by the Nazis, had its own internal system run by prisoners. In the camp, besides our prisoner clothes, we also had a reverse mohawk since we were shaved down the middle of our heads. Once I was able to work, I was given the job of caring for pigs. I worked near the Płaszów train station tending pigs for the SS with another boy. This

17. Jewish cemetery burial house, 1930s (Muzeum Historyczne Miasta Krakowa)

was not a bad job. We ate some of the food that was given to the pigs because we were hungry. And I brought back to the camp some of the food for pigs, or scraps and leftovers from the Nazi's meals, sharing it with my uncle and others.

After about five months, Julag I was liquidated and we were all sent back to Płaszów.[37] Once there, I was reunited with my father.

My uncle came too. But, as my brother Sam remembers, the SS started saying that they wanted volunteers to go to another camp where there was good food and easy work. 'Anyone that goes is going to receive a large loaf of bread', – usually the loaf of bread was round and big – 'oh, and margarine too, and some jam.' And that was such a tempting offer to people who were starving, that they didn't consider anything and went. My uncle volunteered and he was taken out of the camp.

I heard that they were brought through a gate and into an execution pit.

The Płaszów Camp, Fall 1943
You can enter the site of the former Płaszów camp by way of Jerozolimska Street. Jerozolimska Street, or Jerusalem Street, led to the two Jewish cemeteries which were destroyed and on which a part of the Płaszów labor camp was built. We will come to them later.

18. Destruction of the burial house, 1944 (courtesy Meir Eldar and Yad Vashem)

At the beginning of Jerozolimska Street, past an old house and after the second speed bump, is approximately where the main outer camp gate existed. Here, on the left, still stand the buildings used by the camp telephone and radio office (204): Jerozolimska Street 10.

Before the main gate were train tracks and two station

buildings (202, 203). This is the place from which my father, brothers, and I were sent in trains to Mauthausen concentration camp.

Immediately after the main gate, inside on the left, is a two-story house (155), built before the war. It was used as the camp communication office where messages were broadcast through a series of loudspeakers placed all over the camp. During the *Aktionen*, music was played. Next to this building were the barracks for the majority of the German, Latvian and Ukrainian camp guards (M163). As well as rooms for the guards, this building contained a kitchen, dining room and a weapon-storage area.

A little further along, on the right, was where the New Cemetery burial house society building stood (164), between Jerozolimska Street 14 and Abrahama Street 1. During the time of the camp, it was used by the Nazis as a stable for horses and other animals. After it became too small for keeping animals, it was blown up. A film exists of this. First the right wing of this monumental Byzantine-style building was destroyed for the introduction of a railway line to assist with incoming transports and deportations. Then the centre building was blown up. That week the *Kommandant* threw a party to celebrate the destruction of Jewish culture. The left wing remained, even after the war, because the camp's water pump was located in the building's cellar, though it, too, was eventually destroyed.

The Grey House

Continuing up Jerozolimska Street you will see a grey house (171), Jerozolimska Street 3, on the right at the crossroads. This building once served as home to the Jewish burial society. But during the time of the camp, SS men Albert Huyar, Zdrojewski, Landsdorfer, Eckert and Glaser lived in this building. In its basement, many people were murdered or tortured in medieval cells like the *Stehbunker* (standing cell), where you could neither stand straight nor sit down. Beside the house was an inner camp gate leading to the main prisoner barracks.

Płaszów was chosen as the site for a compulsory labor camp in October 1942, under the direction of the Nazi commander *SS Unterstúrmführer* Goeth. The architect Lukas, from Vienna, drew plans for an initial eighty-eight barracks intended for 2,000 to 4,000 prisoners. The engineer Jakub Stendig was placed in charge of construction.[38] In the end, there were 180 barracks, built by the camp's prisoners, for an estimated 24,000 prisoners, workshops and camp guards. Surrounded by double, 3-meter-high electrified fences of barbed wire and guard towers equipped with machine guns, the camp covered an area of about 200 acres (81 hectares).

19. Main entrance of Płaszów concentration camp [marked on map as 202 and 203] (Instytut Pamięci Narodowej)

11 Daily life in Płaszów: Jews and others in the camp

Jews made up the largest number of prisoners in the camp. Jews from all over Europe were brought to the camp: 2,000 from the Tarnów ghetto located east of Kraków, and 6,000 to 8,000 from Hungary. Approximately 35,000 to 50,000[39] people passed through the gates of Płaszów, and many thousands of people were sent from here to other camps for labor and extermination. Between May and June 1944, shortly before the camp's liquidation, the population of the camp had increased to between 22,000 and 24,000.[40] Many of the prisoners died as a result of the combination of hunger, diarrhea, hard labor, diseases, and punishment beatings which we endured. Many others were simply executed.

The camp was initially a labor camp (*Arbeitslager*), then a *KZ* (*Zwangsarbeitslager*) slave-labor camp for Jews and Poles. Prior to the liquidation of the Podgórze ghetto, there were approximately 2,000 prisoners. After the ghetto liquidation, 6,000 Jews were added to the camp's prisoners. From June 1943, the Germans created a separate part of the camp for non-Jewish prisoners. This subsection of the camp housed Polish political prisoners and those accused of minor misdemeanors. Some of these prisoners were set free, though many others were sent to other labor camps in Germany. The number of Polish non-Jews in the camps is estimated at around 4,000, a figure that includes several dozen Romany families who were barracked in a separate compound for Gypsies.[41]

At first, around 1,000 Polish non-Jews were in the camp, held in the *Polenlager* barracks, identified by the letter 'P' sewn on their uniforms. Poles did not stay long in the camp, sometimes weeks or only hours. They were usually quickly sent to labor

20. Płaszów concentration camp (Instytut Pamięci Narodowej)

21. Płaszów concentration camp: to the right are the remains of the burial house (Instytut Pamięci Narodowej)

camps in Germany or released if they were in the camp for small offences. Those who remained worked at the camp *Kartoffel-Keller*, a potato cellar. Polish prisoners, unlike Jewish prisoners, were not allowed to work outside the camp. The serious 'offenders', Polish political prisoners, including alleged members of the *Armia Krajowa*, or national resistance movement, were killed and cremated on Chujowa Górka (206).[42]

Later, during the spring of 1944, three truckloads full of people were brought to Płaszów. They were mainly Poles, members of the *Hasło* underground group who had been betrayed by informers.[43] On 6 August , less than a week after the Warsaw Uprising in August 1944,[44] over 7,000 civilians were arrested in Kraków in order to prevent a similar insurrection from happening, which made a total number of around 10,000 Polish prisoners in the Polish sector of the camp. This day became known as Black Sunday.

At the same time, trainloads of Poles were taken from their jobs and ordered to dig trenches to serve as tank traps to slow down the approaching Soviet Army. Over a period of several weeks, around one hundred Poles were sent from the camp to the Montelupich[45] prison and subsequently transported to Auschwitz. The remaining thousands were released after a week or so.[46] Even though the end of the war was in sight, German tanks were brought into the streets of Kraków and people were arrested to prevent civil resistance.

The camp's food rations

The daily food ration in Płaszów was one kilo of bread (just over two pounds) for around six to eight people, and a tiny piece of butter. This accompanied watery soup with some buckwheat groats (*kasza*) and, occasionally, sauerkraut, fish entrails, or *kogel-mogel*, a kind of custard.

At its height, three ovens produced 6,000 loaves a day to feed 24,000 prisoners: a ration of 250 grams per person per day.[47] It was at this time that an observer from the International Red Cross inspected the camp to make sure that no serious violations of prisoners' human rights were occurring. When

22. Camp commandant Amon Leopold Goeth's Red Villa [178 on map, illus. no. 16] (Sakiewicz)

23. Women working on the *Mannschaftszug* (Instytut Pamięci Narodowej)

he questioned the worker at the bakery (38) how much bread per day each prisoner received, Amon Goeth, the camp commander, standing behind the inspector, raised two fingers to help the baker supply the desired answer.[48]

Prisoners not given work were forced to starve. No work, no food. Dr Władysław Sztencel and some of the camp prisoners did whatever they could, even if very little, to assist them. Sztencel paid for this with his life, shot by SS man Zdrojewski.[49]

I remember I was always dreaming of food, never imagining there could be enough food in the world to satisfy my hunger.

Amon Leopold Goeth – Death-camp commandant

Continue straight approximately 40 meters past the cross-roads to the Red Villa (178) at Heltmana Street 22, a continuation of Jerozolimska Street, where the camp's commandant Amon Leopold Goeth lived. Goeth, a founding mastermind of the Austrian National Socialist Party, was sent to Kraków after having successfully led exterminations in other ghettos. Goeth was arrested and charged in late 1944 by the SS tribunal for corruption and embezzlement, having personally profited from Jewish belongings looted by Nazis and kept in storehouses (85, 88 and 195).[50] Although Goeth was partly reprimanded by the Nazis for breaking their code of subservience to the Reich, he was not fittingly punished until his execution on 13 September 1946.

One of Goeth's innovations to increase labor was the *Mannschaftszug*, which he invented with building supervisor Scheidt. Dump trucks, each of which held two tons of stone, wheeled on narrow-gauge rails, were used day and night to haul building materials from the stone quarry (S) for the construction of buildings, streets and roads. Although named Manpower Troop, the *Mannschaftszug* was comprised of three carts dragged by two columns of thirty-five women on each side. A rope, 100 meters long, was attached to their arms. As they walked, it was wrapped around their bodies, so that they could pull the load with their entire undernourished and weak bodies. Each group had to perform for a twelve-hour shift, moving fifteen loads until they were replaced by the next group of women. Polish women worked during the day, Jewish women during the night. This, according to Goeth, increased labor output, instilled discipline, and served the goal of excellence. Because of such accomplishments, Goeth was given a two-grade promotion on 1 August 1943 to *Obersturmführer*.

Goeth also designed a crematorium (K). Fortunately, however, this particular project was never completed since a part was not available.

12 My brother Sam's encounter with Goeth

My eldest brother Sam told me that he remembers Goeth coming toward him once when he was working with a shovel in the camp. Goeth rode on a horse accompanied by his two Great Danes, Rolf and Ralf, who had to be addressed by prisoners as *Herr*. Goeth had trained them to attack when he cried '*Jude*!' He did this when he passed Sam, even though my brother had done nothing, urging his dogs to attack. The type of scene that followed obviously amused men like Goeth. What happened was that one of the dogs started biting Sam, in his side, above his hips. Even so, Sam tried to keep working and not respond. Eventually, Goeth called the dogs off. Sam knew that Goeth regularly shot those he had set the dogs on. So Sam was lucky. He knew what had been at stake, but he had survived. He had not reacted by trying to defend himself. It was for this reason his life had been spared. It was a kind of test that Goeth put people to.

Goeth was not by any means an exception. There were many like him. One of the cruellest of *Kapos* in the camp was Erik Fehringer.[51] The *Kapos* were mostly German criminals who had been sent from prisons in the camps to work for the SS. Fehringer had murdered both his parents, which is why he was known as 'the orphan'. Another, whom we knew only by the name Willi, a young SS man who had lost his left arm at the front, was one of the most gruesome killers in the camp. Once he said to my brother Nathan, 'You see this whip. Take it and lash the man in front of you twenty times.' Nathan had no choice. People were being shot for absolutely nothing. So he whipped the man, even though he was his friend. Once he was done, Willi said to the other man, 'Look what he has done to you. You want to do that back. You want revenge.'

So he did. He whipped Nathan. He had to.

Turn back and return to the crossroads by the grey house and walk on the path to the left, beside the house marked Jerozolimska Street 3. During the camp's existence, there was an inner camp gate here. The path is unmarked but formerly it was named Abrahama Street. You are now on the path that was the main road inside the camp.

Monument to the thirteen Poles executed in 1939
On the right before the hill is a small monument, erected in 1984, in memory of the thirteen Poles who were executed in 1939, the first victims in Kraków of Nazi murder.

The caves
Continue past several cave entrances on the left. The caves were dug by prisoners. These were intended as an air raid shelter. In front of them was the Nazi officers' camp brothel (173), where Polish camp prisoners were forced to serve the Germans' whims.[52]

24. Memorial to the 13 Poles executed here in 1939 (Sakiewicz)

About thirty to forty feet (ten metres) past the first monument, there is a narrow footpath on the left. Walk up the steep path to the top of the hill. Stop at the top and look. Here you will see a larger view of the camp territory extending across the valley to the treeline at the hill's summit. Beyond the treeline is a stone quarry designated by the Nazis for those chosen for 'special' punishment. The treeline, the visible pylon line to the left, and the apartment blocks to the right, roughly mark out the camp's boundaries. Now it's all grassland, but evidence of the barracks and the industrial plants is still visible.

In the valley and to the right of the path on the nearby hill is the site of the destroyed Jewish cemetery, on which part of the camp was built. Here, today, there is only one recognizable headstone remaining. On it is the name Jakub Chaim Abrahamer, who died in 1932, the great-grandfather of the artist and former actress Roma Ligocka, cousin of the celebrated film director Roman Polański.

Site of former cemeteries (additional walk)
Should you choose to walk on the site of the former cemeteries, take the path to the right past the Grey House.

The camp was built on two cemeteries divided by Jerozolimska Street and the surrounding buildings and land. Cmentarz Podgórski, entered by Jerozolimska Street 25, dates from 1887. The second one, Krakowski Cmentarz, was built in 1932. It was entered from Abrahama Street 3. Respectively, they were approximately five and twenty acres (two and eight hectares) in area. The latter has a five-acre (two-hectare) reserve. The two together total around thirty acres (twelve hectares). There were three buildings, each with cupolas.

These were the cemetery houses or *Beit Tahara*. Recognized in the Jewish religion as holy places, the Old Cemetery burial houses were turned into a bathhouse (49) and delousing (*Entlausung*) station (50).

Please remind yourself that here you are walking on a

25. The one remaining grave in the former Płaszów Jewish cemetery (Sakiewicz)

place where gravestones were crushed into gravel and people were killed and burned. My paternal grandfather and other members of my family had been buried here.

My brothers Sam and Nathan were two of the workers who had to destroy the cemetery. Sam told me he remembered seeing our grandfather's grave being destroyed.

The buildings were destroyed. All the territory of the Jewish cemetery was turned into the concentration camp. The camp roads were paved with Jewish gravestones, which Jewish workers from the ghetto had been forced to destroy to make way for the new camp. The Germans made them dig through the remains of the buried.

Go back to the main path, the old Abrahama Street. From there, go to the top of the steep hill in front of you, taking the secondary path that goes off from the left of Abrahama Street.

13 Duties and 'Health':
Appelplatz – the roll-call square

The Płaszów camp was divided into five main parts: a guard block, including several buildings near the main entrance and officers' villas, the prisoner barracks, the administrative buildings, the industrial buildings (*Neue Gelände*), and the mass grave.

At the centre of the camp was the roll-call square, the *Appelplatz,*[53] where there was a large gallows intended for the regular *Strafappel* (punishment and execution roll-calls) that camp prisoners were forced to witness. This was where prisoners had to assemble in silence twice daily (6 am and 6 pm) at the call of the trumpet, played by Wiluż Rosner.[54] The funeral home of the Old Jewish Cemetery was situated at the right-hand corner of the *Appelplatz*. Whereas back in the ghetto we had watches, clocks, calendars, and glimpses of the German newspapers, in Płaszów we had only the sound of a trumpet to regulate our lives. Only the seasons helped us to determine roughly what time of year it was and how much time had passed since we had been sent there from the ghetto. I recall the endless hours of being on the *Appelplatz* and standing on dead feet next to my father, not always being aware of all the horrors going on around my father and me. I remember believing that a bullet could not penetrate me if I closed my eyes.

Accommodation barracks and the camp uniform
The living quarters of the camp were enclosed within barbed wire for separating women (Z), men (N), and Polish (non-Jewish) prisoners.

Each camp division had its own *Kapo*, as well as a large

26. Workers, Płaszów concentration camp (Instytut Pamięci Narodowej)

number of guards, while barracks, each supervised by its specified elder, housed three tiers of bunks, a stove and a pail of water. The fifty or so barracks, each measuring 14.6 by 8.2 meters, were each meant to hold 150 to 200 people, but more than twice that number must have been crammed in when the camp was full.

The camp uniform was simple: striped, made of thin material under which we were not allowed to wear anything else. To every uniform was added a specific prisoner number and a triangle, coloured to denote the different types of prisoner: red for political prisoners who stayed in the camp, yellow for those working outside the camp, green for criminal prisoners, purple for religious dissidents.

Prisoners discovered wearing clothes underneath their uniforms were executed. A special brutality was practised against women. If someone was found to be wearing a bra, she would have her breasts painted with red lacquer.[55]

It may be hard to imagine as you look at the site of the camp today, but there were some 200 barracks and other buildings. There were roads built, buildings erected for housing, production barracks, and the storage of property looted from the Jews of Kraków. Electricity cables and sewerage pipes were installed as well as latrines, buildings for the police, and accommodation buildings for German officers and their families. There was even a bakery and a brothel. To begin with there was such a shortage of water that, finally, water tanks were built. Before this, however, it was said that Goeth had a swimming pool built for his private use.

The camp infirmary

There was also a camp infirmary (21, 22 and 29). In spite of the attempts of Dr Aleksander Bieberstein and several others, it was not a hospital in the true sense. Rather, it served as a place for isolating diseases as well as a station for those who were to be killed during the next *Aktion*.

Dr Maks Blanke was in charge of the infirmary. He lived with the chief woman warden, *Oberaufseherin* Elsa Ehrich. Blanke's qualification as *Oberarzt* (head doctor of the camp), was his experience as chief of the crematorium at Majdanek extermination camp. Among others working at the infirmary were SS-*Oberscharführer* Hermann Büttner and the Jewish Dr Gross. Under the *Kommandant's* orders, Gross made several of the selections of his fellow Jewish camp prisoners.[56] When the camp was liquidated he was sent to Auschwitz where his son perished. Tragically, Gross was tried and hanged after the war for acting as a Nazi collaborator.[57]

Büttner was an SS man who actually had empathy and never did anything to harm Jewish prisoners. He was probably unique. After the war, Büttner was released due to witnesses testifying to his decent behaviour.[58]

When a selection was announced, everyone thought only how to survive it. Płaszów was much worse than the ghetto. Even so, it seems that some prisoners thought that to be included on a selection might improve matters. Whether this was just a misguided hope, against everything they had already experienced, or they had simply had enough of camp life, I do not know. A few tried to escape the selection lists through blackening their hair with pieces of burned cork, or reddening their cheeks with chicory paper dye, while some managed to bribe the guards. All the same, those chosen for selection were the sick and ones who had grown old, many having prematurely aged because of the workload. No one who saw this process more than once thought that these poor men and women were being sent for any other kind of so-called 'treatment' than death, which, ultimately, was the Nazis' planned destiny for every one of us 'inferior beings'.

A 'health roll-call', 7 May 1944
One cold morning, on 7 May 1944, Goeth staged a 'health roll-call', where, among other things, he spoke about arranging a supplement of 'vitamins' for prisoners who felt weak and introducing a regime of 'work according to ability'.[59] Dr Blanke was placed in charge of the selection between those he considered healthy enough to continue to work and live, and those to be sent to the extermination camps. Every male prisoner – at that time around 20,000 – had to run past Blanke who stood on a small raised platform wearing a big, white fur coat. With a thin stick he waved and pointed, like a manic orchestral conductor, either left or right to mark each individual's fate, whether they were to remain in the camp or be shipped in cattle cars to Auschwitz. In this way, approximately 1,500 were selected.[60]

So, in the days of the camp, dying in bed was a kind of luxury for prisoners. Those with infectious diseases were sent to barrack numbers 1 and 4, where they were 'cured' through an injection of benzene or gasoline.

The camp had electrified barbed-wire fences, and watch-towers, each equipped with a machine gun, telephone, searchlight and loudspeaker. Guards frequently shot at prisoners for 'sport' on the grounds of alleged bread trade. There were also one-level towers for the Jewish *Ordnungsdienst* police force (14). A 15-meter watchtower, equipped with a heavy machine gun and a revolving search-light, watched over the entire area. The camp was equipped with pits where thousands of Jews remaining in the Kraków Ghetto were murdered, after which dense black smoke-clouds smothered the camp with the unforgettable sickeningly sweet smell of incinerated human flesh. Hundreds of men and women were executed: Polish Christians who fought against the Nazis, Jews found in hideouts or caught with false papers, Jewish collaborators with their families, and the German criminal prisoners brought to serve as *Kapos* in the camp.

14 Barrack 82: My work in the camp

In Płaszów, I worked with my father in a shoe factory.[61] We worked in barrack number 82, as marked on the map: on the left side of Abrahama Street, opposite the *Appelplatz*. We were forced to make boots for the German army. Other prisoners' skills were similarly used: tailors for uniforms, printers for publishing bureaucratic forms, propaganda, and notices of death sentences. This we did, although we made boots in such a way that the heel would break off. This was our means of sabotage. Usually, two people worked on one pair of boots. I worked with my father. In the boots we made a hidden cut behind where the heel was to be. We did this so you could not see it from the outside. But it was a defect. So, when a soldier runs, the heel would break off. It made running a little harder. It didn't fall off. But it was broken so that water, snow, or whatever, came in. Since people were shot for this sort of act, we later only damaged one boot per pair. We never stopped our sabotage. That was our part in the resistance.

I recall the fear when SS men came into the shoe production barrack, for fittings for some of the special high riding boots or other shoes we made to order. We had to be always on alert. My father did most of the work to fulfill our quota. He kept me alive not only on the *Appelplatz* and barracks, but also through having me work with him in making German army boots.

The view from my workplace
We were not very far from one of the main execution pits and saw people being chased by the SS through a ditch. We heard

27. *Appelplatz*, Płaszów concentration camp (Instytut Pamięci Narodowej)

28. My workplace, Barrack 82 (Instytut Pamięci Narodowej). Photograph taken from in front of ul. Bergenstrasse (ul. Abrahamer), between a fire pond and Barrack 82, looking down toward the women's barracks (Z); see illus. no.16

the shootings. Soon after the executions the bodies were burned. Workers had to haul wood for the pyres. The wind often carried the smoke in our direction and, with it, the stench of human flesh burning, something I will never forget.

I remember truckloads of people being driven every day by the shoe factory in Płaszów. And as they disappeared over the hill, I heard gunshots. Once I was curious. One day, after the shooting had ended I went to the top of the hill and discovered corpses and firewood stacked up and burning.

Horror, revulsion and fear overwhelmed me.

I lived in Płaszów in dread of death every moment yet still with the will to live. We ate, we worked, and we kept up the score of those murdered each day – the zero always on our side. That was the kind of world in which we had to live. But still we lived.

Only once did I ever hear of someone escaping and not getting caught. But that was years later from another survivor, Mike Staner. He recalls one man, Warenhaupt, a former Maccabi Jewish sports-team ski champion, who was assigned to work on the commandant's car. Instead, he climbed in, left the camp, and was gone. Never heard of again.

News of his escape was greeted by smiles among the prisoners. Sadly, it was an exception to the life we led – if it could be considered life.

15 Mass murder and execution protocol: The camp Kindergarten, 11 March– 14 May 1944

Goeth had established a camp Kindergarten on 11 March 1944. With all the incoming transports to Płaszów, including those from the German invasion of Hungary (occupied since 19 March 1944) and Czechoslovakia, more and more children were added to the prisoners of the camp. Few remained in the camp for long. Some people paid large bribes to keep their children. Only *OD* Jewish Ghetto Police members and similar officials were allowed to bring their children into the camp. As before in the ghetto, parents were persuaded to send their children to the camp's Kindergarten. In front of the newly-built block, a playground was set up, with lawns and rows of flowers – things that had become almost unimaginable following the long months of a life comprising forced labor, exhaustion and virtual starvation.

On 14 May, at the time of the usual morning *Zählappel* (roll-call), loudspeakers around the camp were playing German children's songs, perhaps to keep the children calm, but perhaps also as part of the guards' sense of 'humour', knowing that the children's parents would know what was really taking place. The lullabies *Mama, komm zurück; Gut nacht Mutti;* and *Mami, kauf mir ein Pferdchen* (*Mother, come back; Goodnight Mommy;* and *Mama, buy me a pony*) accompanied the transport of nearly 300 children, and some sick people, to the slaughterhouse Auschwitz, all led there in rows of five by *Tatele* Koch, a good *OD* man.[62] Out of all the children, only about twenty were saved through hiding in the latrines under the excrement.

That day, Goeth cabled Auschwitz and demanded *Sonderbehandlung* (special treatment) for this transport, with no *Selektion* allowed. In other words, deportation to the gas chambers without any reprieve for those fit enough to work.[63] Around 1,400 people were deported that day.[64]

The Jews from Hungary, mid-1944

Since the time when Płaszów was turned into a concentration camp, all executions had to be sanctioned first by headquarters in Berlin. Goeth continued carrying on murdering and robbing his prisoners as before, although now it had to be documented and approved by his senior authorities. In mid-1944, when the outcome of the war was already decided – the Russians were already in Lwów, the Allies in Normandy and the south of France – the concentration camp administration in Berlin (*Amtsgruppe D*) asked Goeth provisionally to accommodate in Płaszów around 10,000 Jewish prisoners from Hungary, because of a lack of space in Auschwitz. Goeth agreed but under the condition that he could carry out a *Selektion* to eradicate all 'non-productive elements' in the camp. He received the go-ahead.

The Hungarian Jews arrived; women with shaved heads, clothed in garments that looked like flour sacks with slits for the head and arms, had been sent from the Budzyń labor camp.

Within a few weeks of their arrival at Płaszów, at the beginning of August, they were transported again – to Auschwitz.[65] The momentary lack of accommodation there had been resolved. The gas chambers were operating at their optimum level.

Goeth's final selection, August 1944

In August 1944, Goeth wanted to rid himself of some of the 'old-timers' – veteran camp prisoners who had witnessed his murders and corruption. One man was an engineer named

Popper. He was a foreman at the electric plant. He knew too much about Goeth, however. When his name was added to the list of people to be sent to their deaths, Popper asked Goeth to spare his life. *'Du hast schon genug gelebt,'* Goeth replied ('You have lived long enough').[66] The killing took place on 13 August 1944.

That day, both Wilek Chilowicz, the chief officer (*Lagerälterste*) of the camp *OD*; his nephews; his deputy, Mieczysław Finkelstein; and *OD* officer Faerber, were also killed, along with Chilowicz's wife and several close collaborators, to eliminate further witnesses to Goeth's actions. Goeth did not try to conceal the murders. Instead, he made everyone in the camp march past and gaze at the sign above the bodies propped up on tables set in the middle of the *Appelplatz*: 'These bandits were armed and wanted to incite a prisoners' riot.'[67]

Goeth had set them up. Creating a false escape plan in which the group would be caught and shot, he thereby got over the hurdle of having to provide Berlin with reasons for their execution. What Goeth was trying to hide was that he had used his willing accomplices to help plunder for himself Nazi stolen goods and sent them to Czechoslovakia for storage. But Goeth was arrested the same day. After the initial hearings he was imprisoned in Vienna. He was replaced immediately at Płaszów by SS-*Sturmführer* Grum, then, several weeks later, by SS-*Oberscharführer* Schupke.[68]

The two mass execution sites

Continuing along the camp path will lead you to the southeastern part of the camp. Here is situated a large cross in memory of the many Poles who were killed at this spot. Prisoners named it *Chujowa Górka* [69] (206), or Prick Hill, a derogatory pun on the name of SS man Albert Huyar.

The camp's two mass graves (marked on Bau's SS camp map as circles numbered 206 and 207) had been Austrian artillery stand dugouts in the mid-nineteenth century. In September 1944, the Nazis tried to remove all traces of the

29. Site of mass execution [206 on map; see illus. no. 16] (Sakiewicz)

30. Monument to the victims [207 on map; see illus. no. 16] (Sakiewicz)

mass murder that had occurred here, ordering remaining prisoners to dig up and burn the bodies of those victims not already cremated.

Joseph Bau writes that victims were made to undress and lay side by side on the tree branches they had been made to place there. Then they were shot. One group laid logs down on the corpses before they too were shot. The last group had to pour oil and gasoline and immolate those who had been killed, prior to their own deaths. No one could utter a sound since the Germans had taken care to plug their mouths with plaster. All clothing and possessions were kept for the benefit of the self-proclaimed *Übermenschen*. Before being burned the bodies were examined for dental gold, or for money or valuables in any bodies which were still clothed. The killing was completed with the bodies or ashes being covered with earth, through the use of the camp tractor.[70]

It is estimated that between 8,000 and 12,000 people[71] were murdered at these two areas. Yet Płaszów was considered just a small camp.

Walk to the right on the asphalt path toward the three other monuments. These are situated beside the circular ditch: the mass execution pit in which thousands of people, mostly Jews including members of my family, were murdered. The first smaller monument on the right, at the end of the road, is one placed by the Jewish community of Kraków. It reads:

> In this place in the years 1943–1945 several thousand Jews from Poland and Hungary were murdered and their remains cremated.
>
> We do not know the names of the murdered ones but we do know that they were Jews. In this place human speech does not have words to describe the incredible bestiality, suffering and cruelty. But we do know that it was committed under Hitlerism.
>
> In memory of those whose last screams exist as silence in this Płaszów cemetery and who were murdered under the Fascist pogroms.

A smaller monument was placed near the large monument in 2000 in memory of the Hungarian Jewish women who were prisoners of Płaszów concentration camp before being sent to the gas chambers of *KL* Auschwitz-Birkenau.

The largest of the three monuments, depicting five burdened people with broken hearts, was erected in 1964 during Poland's era of Soviet communist rule. The legend on the back of the monument neglects to mention that the camp's victims were mainly Jews. This monument marks Lipowy Dołek[72] (207) where executions of camp and political prisoners from surrounding towns and villages took place.

16 The liquidation of the Płaszów camp, Fall 1944

The liquidation of *KL* Płaszów began gradually, as early as July 1944, as the Soviet and Allied-controlled Polish armies drew closer to the eastern border. By then, the total camp population had risen to over 20,000. The camp could boast of an international population, including prisoners from Italy and Hungary as well as Jews, Poles and Romanies.

By the fall, most of the men were sent to Mauthausen concentration camp in Austria, Gross-Rosen concentration camp west of Wrocław, Flossenbürg in Germany, and a few for labor at Oskar Schindler's factory in Brünnlitz, Czechoslovakia. Women were largely sent to Ravensbrück or Auschwitz-Birkenau. In October, a transport of between 3,000 to 5,000 people, mainly young girls, a large number of them from Kraków, were transported from Auschwitz to Stutthof, near Gdańsk. The train reached the coast. There, the SS put them on a ship that they scuttled in mid-ocean, drowning all but a few in the Baltic Sea.[73]

In an attempt to remove any evidence of the extent of the inhuman crimes that had taken place at Płaszów, some prisoners were kept to dig up and burn the bodies of people shot by the Nazis. Sometimes people found the bodies of their friends or members of their own families. The entire camp area was dismantled. From 27 August, all the wooden barracks were taken apart and, together with camp records, the remaining prisoners sent to other camps. After 15 October, the date of one of the last large transports with 1,600 prisoners transported to Gross-Rosen, approximately 600 people remained at the camp. This included 160 female and 40 male German *Kapos*[74] to complete the liquidation. The last transport[75] of prisoners left the Płaszów camp three days prior to the Red Army liberation of Kraków on 18 January 1945.

PART III

Auschwitz and the Process of Healing, 1944–Present

17 Auschwitz-Birkenau after Płaszów: A brief visit to the beautiful flatlands of Austria

After the Płaszów camp was liquidated, my father, brothers and I were transported by train to a place by the River Danube. Although it was my first trip abroad, it was unfortunately not our captors' plan to take us on a romantic tour of the Austrian flatlands. Where we ended up was Mauthausen concentration camp. From Kraków, it's a distance of approximately 500 kilometers, give or take 100 kilometers. So, if you can imagine: we were in Kraków, in the Płaszów camp, and then put in the crowded and confined space of a cattle wagon for three-and-a-half days and nights to Mauthausen. There, my brothers were taken off to work in the quarry, but my father and I were sent back east within a week to Auschwitz – about 50 kilometers west of Kraków.

Auschwitz-Birkenau, 24 August 1944
I remember it was night when we pulled in; straight away, there was a weird sound that we heard, and strange smells that I noticed. Through the bars of our cattle car I could see immense fires on the distant horizon and an enormous amount of smoke.

All of a sudden the train stopped and we started hearing voices and dogs barking; but the doors were not opened and so we were left there.

Little did we know that the short track on which our wagon was standing completed a network of tens of thousands of miles of railroads that spanned Eurasia and the Mediterranean, stretching from Norway in the north to Athens in the south,

31. Auschwitz-Birkenau (Bernard Offen)

ultimately connecting hundreds of thousands of people from numerous countries to a shared predestined fate at what was for so many, quite literally, the end of the line. We had arrived at the greatest of the Nazi's numerous killing grounds.

In the morning, the wagon doors opened up, and some people ran in to the wagons, by then awash in human waste. They were wearing striped uniforms; they were prisoners. They were shouting and beating us to get out of the cattle cars fast, no matter that we had been jammed in a suffocatingly hot mobile jail cell for three-and-a-half days, which for some had already proven a death sentence. Now, roused from our nightmare, there was a huge amount of fear and confusion. My father and I got off the wagon quickly, where the new camp's prisoners started to line us up on what turned out to be the Auschwitz-Birkenau selection ramp.

From that group of humanity lined up on the selection ramp, we were gradually driven in one direction toward a group of SS men who decided whether it was going to be life or death that met each new arrival. Consequently, with either their palm or a stick, they casually waved this way, to the right, or that way, to the left.

After the selection, I saw my father moving away in the opposite direction. To the left. We didn't know which direction was good and which was bad. We just had no idea. I was told to go over to the right, so I did. But just before the gate, which is still there today, I turned around as we were being chased and saw my father standing in a group of people. And, from a distance, we just looked at each other. We still didn't know; I didn't know that I would survive and he wouldn't. But I sensed that we would not see each other again. We had eye contact for a moment. Then I was marched past the gate to be showered and tattooed.

My father was murdered, in one of the large gas chambers. He went one way, following the selection, and I the other. I'm here because I went to the right.

When I got off the train, before I went up in front of the SS men for the selection, a prisoner had told my father, in either Yiddish or Polish, to tell me to lie about my age. 'Get behind me, and stand on your toes', my father instructed me. This is what saved me at the selection: the fact that I lied about my age. When there was no selection, men, women, and children went straight to the gas chambers. It all depended on their need for slave labor. Simply that.

Oddly enough, I literally forgot my birth date. So I have three different dates, which are in my records in Auschwitz. And until about 1992, I was living under both the wrong birth date and the wrong year. I was two years older than I thought. It did mean I got my social security earlier than I expected ...

Looking at Auschwitz-Birkenau today, you see a lot of grass and, as a consequence it looks quite peaceful in some ways. But back then, there wasn't one piece of grass that existed within our reach. If there had been, we would have eaten it! Any grass that did remain was all trodden down: there was just either mud or dust. It's also quiet, the silence almost mocking the memory I have of the terror that filled Auschwitz-Birkenau not so long ago.

The Gas Chambers

The Nazis took precautions to keep the mass slaughter a secret. The gas chamber and crematorium crews, called the *Sonderkommando*, were regularly slaughtered and replaced.

Whereas Płaszów concentration camp never had its planned furnace for getting rid of prisoners, Auschwitz-Birkenau could boast that it had six, operating in a simple, direct and highly efficient way: four crematoria with gas chambers, two gas chambers in converted farmhouses, and cremation pits and pyres. Just one of them had the capacity to gas 3,000 people at once. And the Nazis did this many, many times, often around the clock. About a million people were killed this way.

According to a *Sonderkommando* survivor I once spoke with, it worked like this: people came in from the undressing rooms where they had been told to keep their clothes together. 'Don't get them mixed up', they were told, 'Everything's going to be all right'. It was just going to be the usual delousing and a shower. 'There'll be soup afterwards', or, 'We're looking for shoemakers or carpenters.' All kinds of words they were told, simply as a deception.

And what appeared to be showers *were* there. Indeed, there were showerheads. However, there was no water. That was just a pretence. They squeezed in there approximately three thousand people at a time. Towards the end of these operations, people started panicking, but they pushed them right into the chamber. There were prisoners and SS to push them into the chamber, close the door and within fifteen to twenty minutes they were dead. From outside, near the top of the roof, SS men dropped in the crystal pellets that turned into the gas called *Zyklon-B*.

After all the selected prisoners were dead, they were removed by other prisoners dragging their bodies. There was an electric elevator. On it, bodies were brought up to the level above. They were then dragged along what looks like a sewer ditch. This was wetted down with water so it would be easier to drag the bodies to the ovens. There was one wagon for each of the sets of rails that led to the crematorium ovens. There were about fifteen of those. Although I cannot be certain, I believe that my father died in the one marked KII.

So, within twenty-four hours there wasn't even a trace that a human being had existed. After the ashes were dumped into the ponds nearby, the remaining bones that didn't burn were crushed with hammers by other prisoners.

When I got to my barracks, in the row now marked 'BIIa: Quarantine', I asked other inmates what had happened to my father. And the answer was, 'Well, he went up the chimney.'

Of course, I did not know what that meant until a few days later when other prisoners told me what this meant. It was a kind of camp jargon, which soon became terrifyingly clear.

The building marked 'R: Sauna' is a real shower house. And that's where I was tattooed. Two prisoners grabbed hold of my arms while a third one tattooed on me an identification number: *B-7815*. Though it was painful, it saved my life having a tattoo. If you didn't get a number you were dead. Simple as that. Having the tattoo meant that there was some intention that I was going to be kept for a while and so, in a sense, I was safe – as long as I was useful, that is.

My angels in the Quarantine Camp and a visit from Dr Mengele
I was marched to the Quarantine Camp (marked 'BIIa') after my shower and tattoo. The compound functioned as an isolation area in the camp for men, Jews and non-Jews from different countries, during the period August 1943 to November 1944. The purpose of the quarantine period, apart from identifying those who might have infectious diseases, was to ingrain in new arrivals absolute submission to camp discipline.

I was in barrack number 5, fifth from the compound entrance gate at the far end from the now-infamous guard tower with its fearful arch, 'Death's Gate', through which all the trains passed. As in most of the places I was in, I was protected by some of the others who took care of me. They helped me just by telling me what was the right thing to do:

'Bernard, you go over this way', or sometimes by giving me things: 'Here is an extra piece of bread', or, 'Here is an extra piece of clothing', and, 'You go and sleep up there.'

I was small and skinny, and somehow these men got the idea that they were there to take care of me, which they did. They saved my life. That's why I call them my angels.

From time to time, either an SS man, the block eldest, *Kapo*, or an assistant, came in and told people that another selection was going to happen; they came in and just wrote down tattoo numbers of those who had failed the test, just weren't needed, or whatever; and those whose names were written down were sent away, destined for the gas chamber. On this particular occasion, there was a *Kapo*, a gay man. He was basically a good *Kapo*, which wasn't always the case.

Anyway, he saved my life by telling me that there would be a selection the next day, and in order to have a chance of not being chosen for selection he told me what to do: 'When it is your turn to come up before the SS man, don't just walk up there. Run up there! But don't look him in the eye. Look at his boots. And just stand there smartly, as if you've still got strength.' So, when it was my turn I came up close to the man in charge of the selection, in the way I had been instructed, looked at his boots and waited ... 'OK, that way', he pointed, and everything was all right.

I found out later that the man whose boots I had looked at was Dr Josef Mengele, the notorious doctor, who spent his career selecting people for all sorts of hideous medical experiments, particularly on twins. That's who it turned out to be, but of course, I didn't know anything at the time other than that my luck had not run out. I was still alive.

The other thing that the block eldest did to help me was to get me up on the top bunk. There were three levels of bunks, and the top one was the best place to be, because we all had diarrhea and everything came down. There was virtually no chance that we would make it to the latrine, so that's why we usually had our pants tied at the bottom during the day just to hold all the shit in, as we were beaten for having lost it some place along the way. We were beaten for everything. It was an existence that was unimaginable. Yet, I always, *always* had hope. I saw some people run to the barbed-wire fence who knew they would be electrified when they reached it; in a way, they perhaps welcomed it as they couldn't last any longer. I never considered doing this. Even though my body was in the camp, my mind was elsewhere. I was escaping a lot in my mind, literally out, like an animal able to fly. I projected myself out of the camp as a bird, transcending my body, unerringly. That was part of the intuitive technique that saved my life.

Dachau, October 1944

After just over two months in Auschwitz-Birkenau in 1944, the *Kapo* who had previously protected me told me it would be better for me if I went on a particular transport. I had no choice, of course. So, on 27 October, I followed orders and was taken with others by truck to what I later found out was Landsberg-Kaufering near Munich, a sub-camp of Dachau concentration camp.[76] Once there, I was marched daily to a

32. This is the earliest photograph of me that exists, taken three months after liberation. I was a mascot for an American tank unit (Bernard Offen)

construction site where I was forced to work in the black-smith's shop.

After six months, at the beginning of May 1945, we were put on what later became called a Death March, for if anyone could not keep up, he or she was shot on the spot. I have sometimes wondered why the soldiers who forced us to march kept on going, knowing they were about to lose the war. I can only think that it was because they were trained well – not to think well, but simply to obey and follow orders. That's what good soldiers do. Only bad soldiers would have broken rank! Anyway, after almost a week of marching, we were driven into camp barracks, and the next morning all the guards had gone. Vanished.

Being stronger than the others, I was asked to find out what was happening and to bring help. I was advised to go along the route we marched, because we did not know what was ahead of us. I walked along the edge of the woods because there was fighting still going on. When I saw a tank with a star on it, I was sure it was not German; I thought it could be Russian.

I saw soldiers and I came out with my arms raised. As luck would have it, they turned out to be American soldiers, who I remained with as a mascot for almost two months.

We had marched around fifty kilometers from Landsberg to near Wolfrats-Hausen where we were liberated by the American army on 2 May 1945. The German villagers living around the concentration camps were gathered and forced to look at the corpses and to be witnesses to the horrors.

From my family, only my two brothers and I survived.

When I was liberated, I had turned 16 just a few weeks earlier. In the days after, I remember hearing for the first time the English spoken by Americans. As the unit's mascot, I remember going out once and learning what fishing GI-style is: the soldier told me to duck as he threw several grenades into a stream, after which we watched the stunned fish float to the top.

18 After my liberation: The search for my brothers, 1946

From a list of survivors I saw while in a Munich refugee camp, I found out that my brothers were still alive. My own name did not appear on this list, so they did not know I was alive.

I rode on a coal train to Salzburg the following day, to my brothers' last refugee camp. I had a great determination and vision to find them. They had already left for Italy, however, where they had joined the Polish army. Following their trail through several refugee and army camps – by hitchhiking, walking and riding on trains – it took me more than six months to finally catch up with them in Bari, Italy. The emotional moment of finding and reuniting with them is still imprinted in my heart and mind. Italy became for me the first beautiful land in which my healing began.

After one year in Italy, we went to England, since my brothers were ordered to go there to be discharged from General Anders' army. This was the second stop on the path to America, which always was my dream since watching American movies during my Krakovian childhood. It was a time when the status of the refugee was changing to one of normality. We did not return to Poland, which was now overrun by the Soviets and where it was still not a safe place for Jews to live. In addition to the well-known Kielce pogrom in 1946, one took place in Kraków in August just after the war.[77]

My brothers and I lived with the Lyons and Freedman families during the years I spent in London. They were wonderful people and included me in their extended family, for which I am grateful to this day.

I often skipped school to watch films, as many as four in a

single day. My healing process was watching war films, westerns and lots of comedies. I became the GI soldier or cowboy – but never, never the Indian.

In a sense, I learned more English at the movies than at school. And London was where I had my first paid job, on Gerard Street, near Piccadilly Circus where the famous statue of Eros stands, firing his arrows toward love's destiny. For me, his arrows pointed west, since I constantly dreamed of going to America.

33. Bernard Offen and his brothers, London 1950 (Bernard Offen)

19 Coming to America, 1951

In 1951, the dream became true, my brothers and I left for America, sponsored by some family relatives who had emigrated to America before the First World War. They met us at New York harbor, where we stayed in a hotel – not a common thing for us back then.

In the few days we stayed there we had our first taste of America. Then we headed along the Pennsylvania turnpike to Detroit, where we met all our cousins – fifth cousins, as it happens. Then, in Michigan, I started my new life.

It was just about one year later that I was drafted into the United States army to fight in Korea. So I said goodbye to my brothers, and went by ship to Korea. Toward another war.

I was there seventeen months – seventeen months, ten days and I forget how many hours. But who was counting …? I was. I was counting every minute to get back, although the reason why I wanted to go in the first place was that, unconsciously, I saw myself doing the work of my former liberators. I believed, and passionately felt, that I was somehow defending liberty against the communists. Much later, during the Vietnam War in the 1960s, I rethought my politics.

A normal, everyday nuclear family

In 1957, after returning from Korea, I met my future wife. From our marriage I have two sons, Michael and Jay.

I went into business operating a coin-operated laundry. While my brothers designed and sold clothing, my business was washing them! It was fine.

My desire for a normal life and family was deep. Deep down, I wanted to replace and substitute my American family for my murdered Polish one. So, in the years that followed, I tried to live just a normal life, far away from the realities of war and servitude.

Later, in the 1970s, I began protesting about the nuclear issue after reading a Detroit newspaper article describing the circles of death in an atomic explosion. When I read this report, it became clear to me that atomic bombs were a potential planetary gas chamber, and that we are all exposed to this potential. I remember carrying a placard with my statement:

> As an Auschwitz survivor, number B-7815, I see the neutron bombs as the Zyklon-B of the 1980s. The Nuremberg trials were written to prosecute after the facts became known. Are we going to be able to prosecute anyone for planetary genocide?!

I gradually became very, very angry at the whole world after the war. For a long, long time, I remember this dream: I was Atlas, holding up the world. And I started to shake the world, cursing everything and everyone because of what had happened to me and those around me ... Then I woke up and realized that if I kept shaking the world I would be committing suicide, because I am part of that world. I shook myself awake and shouted: 'Cancel! Cancel! Cancel that dream!'

The nuclear bomb still exists. That we would consider using that for 'defense' is insanity. How did we get to this place?

Many of the people who were Hitler's henchmen grew up in an environment of hatred of Jews. Jews were vermin, something not human. So, to the Germans, it seemed right to kill and mistreat us. It was an OK thing to do. As a matter of fact, not only was it just an OK thing to do. For them, it was a good thing. Some believed that they were doing God's work. And Hitler, to many of them, was like God. I recall thinking: the Germans, with their literature, art and education, are the most civilized people on Earth. So how did the people of Goethe, Beethoven and Schiller end up creating camps as part of a technologically efficient system with gas chambers and crematoriums designed and developed to dispose of millions of people? It is true that people had grown up in intolerance and hatred of Jews for a long time. Maybe it was an easy step to make: to ignore them or erase them in other, more practical ways. And yet, what of humanity?

It is said that Mahatma Gandhi, when once asked what he thought of Western civilization answered that he felt it might be a good idea. No civilized society would tolerate anything I have just mentioned, which is of course only a tiny sample of European history; Western history is even worse.

Often we do not recognize this. And that is the insanity, global insanity, to which I want to address myself: When do we begin to heal from the insanity of not looking at what is happening to people as human beings? How did we grow those Nazis, who willingly threw the *Zyklon-B* pellets into the gas chambers? Thousands killed at a time. Could we do this? I think so. We are capable even of that. For a long time I was denying that I could be capable of doing similar things, but now I do not think this is true. We are all capable of similar things. Under the right circumstances almost anyone can do anything. And circumstances can lead to such things happening, if we do not check ourselves and our values.

Albert Einstein wrote that, following the discovery of nuclear physics, everything had changed in the world – with the exception of mankind. In order to survive, we would have to change too, through changing our minds. Surely, the follies and human-created disasters of the past century are enough to warn us of the nemesis that awaits us or a future generation.

20 The Work: Retirement – I begin my real work

Following selling my business and retiring, I decided to go back to school to learn what I had always wanted to do: to make films. I enrolled in a communications course at Sonoma State University (film being my principal focus), and started work on the first of my three films, *The Work* (1983). This was my first attempt to really confront the past. I gave the film a subtitle: *The work I had to do on myself.* It has a double meaning: the slavery I and thousands of others endured, and the work we all have to do on ourselves if we are going to improve the world we live in. Long ago, I realized that I couldn't change what happened to me, so I have to change myself. This has been the hardest work I have ever had to do.

The film is not simply a documentary. In a sense, it was my own chosen form of therapy, a catharsis of sorts. And although it does represent both personal and historical information, I would rather hope that it acts as a catalyst for internal self-reflection – the subject of my degree thesis, *Self-Determination in the Process of Healing* (International University, Los Angeles, 1987) – and dialogue among those who watch it.

My first return to Poland, 1981

On my way to the 1981 world gathering of Holocaust survivors in Israel, I spent ten days in Poland, in Kraków and Auschwitz. This was the first time that I returned to my birthplace and the killing grounds for millions of Jews. My hometown was familiar, yet changed: The places where I watched soccer games, played hookey from school, and in the winter rode a sled down the hill near where we lived. When I

104

went to the site of Płaszów, I stood again in the place where I witnessed bodies burning on the pyres. I felt the need to be alone.

Having seen my old neighbourhood, the ghetto and the site of the Płaszów camp, I felt ready to return to Auschwitz-Birkenau.

I was never in the main Auschwitz camp, but because of the proximity of Auschwitz I (now a museum) to Birkenau, where I was, I had some vivid flashbacks.

I remembered the train journey: the thirst, the dying and the dead surrounding me. I remembered my father trying to protect me and his feeling of helplessness.

I become an official guest of Auschwitz

The museum director, Kazimierz Smoleń, and historian Teresa Świebocka were extremely willing to help. Teresa spoke English and made me and my companion Annetta feel welcome, making us official guests of the museum.

Ironically, the room we stayed in was Commandant Höss's office. Höss was the commandant of all of Auschwitz, including the factories and extermination centers. Here, Höss and his staff processed the orders for transport, executions, exterminations, and the Auschwitz factory orders for the Nazi war machine. His wife and five children lived in comfort, isolated from the horrors of the camp less than one block away.

'*Arbeit macht frei*' ('Work makes you free'), Höss wrote before his execution in 1947, repeating the words written on the sign above the camp gate: 'Work in prison is a means of training for those prisoners who are fundamentally unstable and who need to learn the meaning of endurance and perseverance.'

Teresa made archive material available to us, including original transport documents. The documents named my father Jacob, my brothers Sam and Nat, a cousin named Aaron, and me. Then we met Odi, who had been a prisoner in the camp. Odi chose to remain there, staying on to work at the

105

Auschwitz Museum after liberation. Odi endured Auschwitz I for four years.

When I asked him why he stayed, he told me that here he did not have dreams about the past: 'On the outside, I would have to pretend and try to be something I am not. I would have to be political in order to get a decent job.'

His window overlooked the remaining gas chamber. Annetta and I went and sat in the gas chamber where we meditated for some time in silence.

I thought about my mother's, sister's and my father's deaths in a gas chamber like this one. This small gas chamber held 800 people at a time.

We also met Berndt who worked at the Auschwitz Museum For Action Reconciliation, educating young Germans who spend a summer at the museum doing volunteer work.

Berndt and I walked to the ruins of the two gas chambers at the end of the Birkenau ramp. Just before the Russians liberated Auschwitz, the Nazis blew up their 'special operations' installations.

Truckloads of ashes were disposed of in the Vistula river. Were my father's ashes washed away in the Vistula, I wondered? Or are they part of the human fertilizer that nourishes the late spring flowers?

For thirty-six years I stuffed down my pains and fears. Living in America, there were still much that I had denied, even to myself, as if it was all a bad dream. I feel that I was an emotional cripple in many ways, not seeing at all the unexpressed pain buried deep within me. I just did not realize that what was running me was not really me, but my emotions; or, rather, my unexpressed emotions. Instead of truly living, I was still in many ways living with fears from my past.

I am not a survivor anymore – something I must not forget if I want to remain free of the debilitating effects of the trauma I suffered as a child.

Even so, having recognized what I must do, it took me

another ten years of reflecting on what I experienced to finally decide to return to Poland again. Since then, I have returned each summer as part of a continuous process of self-confrontation with my memories of the past and the realities of the present. This process is not easy, but necessary for healing my past and achieving reconciliation for the future.

21 My search for meaning

Between then and now, I have been continuing my teaching work and what has been for me a life of learning, through a search for understanding and meaning. Part of that is also the desire for fulfillment in life, and for learning from my own experiences and about others and their lives.

In 1984–85, I spent a year in Israel. It was my second visit there. I enjoyed it very much, being under the sun with friends both old and new. I remember climbing up Mount Sinai with the eminent spiritual mentor, Rabbi Zalman Schachter-Shalomi, up to the place where it is written that Moses received the laws that were needed to guide the former slaves. It's a story I have always thought profound, for even though the slaves were free from Pharaoh's bondage, they still required God's word and guidance to help them understand the world and their part in it. Still true today, of course. We're part of the ongoing struggle to sort out our differences and figure out how to live with each other peacefully and with content. That's how I see things.

After my year in Israel, I went back to my home in quiet and peaceful Middletown, California. I started going on cross-country walks throughout the world. As a member of Global Walkers, my aim has been to share with people my vision of peace. Doing so, I have walked across half the United States and, in 1991, from Kraków to Auschwitz. Walking so much, I really got to see how devastated the environment has become. You don't really see it from a car. You only see it by walking and observing.

Many times, on route, I have lectured at universities, screened my films, and talked about my experiences in

England, Paris and Poland. In Paris, in 1992, I spent a month teaching in conjunction with Clarity Confusion Association, founded by Claire Nuer, a French Jew and hidden child during the Holocaust. By chance, Claire and I found out about each other and our respective experiences; we came to realize that it was likely that I could have been acquainted with Claire's father in the camps. Our trip to Paris provided us with a chance to further explore that connection as well as cope with our loss.

Claire, her family, members of Clarity Confusion and I drove from Paris to Poland to see the site of the former Kraków Ghetto, my birthplace, and the camps I was in, Płaszów and Auschwitz. It was a difficult but healing experience to have a group walking and witnessing with me in the places where my family had suffered.

Children of war: Friends and enemies
A couple of years later, I met with Claire in San Francisco for a panel discussion about conflict and suffering. The four other people on the panel, like Claire and me, were Bay Area residents. All of us had quite different but related roots of trauma. And what was important was that each of us could be labelled 'enemies' of someone else in a group comprising the daughter of a Nazi, a survivor of Hiroshima, a Palestinian refugee, the son of an atom bomb scientist during the Second World War, and me, a survivor of Auschwitz.

The interesting thing was that we had all first met each other over the preceding two years at Claire's seminars, which aimed at improving relationships within families and between communities. During this time, we all became friends.

Barbara, whose father fought in the Viennese underground for the Nazis, had felt so guilty about her father's actions when we first met that she pretended to be Swiss, not German. Fortunately, over time, she learned how to deal better with her guilt.

Zaher, a Palestinian refugee, was 9 years old when his

family left his hometown near Jerusalem after the Six-Day War in 1967. Because of his experiences and what he had been told, Zaher used to blame Jews – all Jews – for all of his problems. 'Every time something went wrong, it was always *their* fault', he said.

Zaher met Claire, who works professionally with medical patients, when his wife discovered she had cancer. When he found out Claire was Jewish, he had to decide whether to support his wife or give in to his old fears and resentments. Thankfully, after some time and consideration, he chose to let go of his prejudices. 'As a victim, I thought I was the only one in the world', he said. 'I'd been carrying the war with me all my life.' Later, Zaher came to Claire's seminars, where I first met him.

Joel, whose father had worked on the Manhattan Project, said that having met the others in the group brought him to believe that war becomes impossible once individuals begin to react on a personal level. Joel sat next to Kumi, who was 3 years old when the atomic bomb was dropped on Hiroshima, eight miles from her home. Hearing Kumi tell her story, Joel said he realized that the justification for dropping the bomb became completely irrelevant because he finally understood the pain of another person. 'I became personally involved', he said.

As Claire said at the end of the meeting, victims can become tyrants if they believe only their versions of the past. There are victims and there are perpetrators and one does not have to forgive the other for their acts. However, if we are going to reconcile our lives with people different from ourselves, then we need to recognize our common shared humanity.

Zen Peacemakers, 1999

In the fall of 1998, I got an e-mail from the Zen Peacemaker Order in Santa Fe, in New Mexico. They invited me to join in a five-day Bearing Witness Retreat at Auschwitz-Birkenau, something they have hosted annually since 1996. This organization is an interfaith network of people and organizations practising a vision of peace through study, spiritual practice and social actions. At Auschwitz-Birkenau, an interfaith assembly of Buddhist monks and teachers, Jewish rabbis, Christian priests and nuns, Sikhs and Sufi imams, and other participants from all around the world, gathered to experience the overpowering anguish and, in a sense, the sacredness of this site.

At the conference, I met Joan Halifax, an anthropologist and Zen priest. Joan had studied healing through her work with men on Death Row in a maximum security New Mexico penitentiary, trying to understand the relationship between victims and victimizers. What Joan saw in many of the prisoners was that even though we use language to express a clear divide between the two, the victimizer and the victim, both can exist in the same person.

Experiencing Auschwitz as a visitor, years after the real suffering took place, Joan recognized that it is only through experience that analysis can come. Seeing young people walking around the camp site made her wonder why they – and anyone else – go there. Maybe they don't know themselves, but since they are the ones who are going to be shaping the future, maybe it's a good thing. Perhaps young people need to touch the roots of suffering – the most inhuman aspect of ourselves – in order to discover our humanity.

Until now, humans have not been very successful dealing with enemies. Whether through fighting them, running away or trying to make friends with them, the results have been usually only temporary. Warfare has not ceased. The world is still full of enemies in spite of all the advanced weapons and technology at our disposal. Maybe we all have to learn how to love our enemies, in order to destroy properly our hypocrisies and our wars, as well as our fears. For what is it we are really protecting ourselves against? Do we really know?

In so many ways, our culture is in a situation of undisclosed grief. We seem to have made ourselves fundamentally numb because the reality we live in is too much to face. Suffering is relative, though each person has his or her own pain, a sustained horror that is something extremely difficult to grasp. Maybe staying too much within the identity of Auschwitz is less than helpful. Maybe that identity has to be transcended in order to be fully healed. Maybe you can't be just a survivor; you have to be more then a survivor. Maybe the survivor has to die. This is why when we ask, 'What happened in the concentration camps of Europe? How could human beings do this to human beings? What's going on today?', then we must go deeper and deeper into these questions. And as we grow and develop, what is revealed is not just a question about what happened at Auschwitz – it's the question of our life.

22 *The passage of trauma*

At the Auschwitz conference, I also met Dr Anna Gamma, who works with traumatized people in Switzerland. With her, I discussed trauma and my experience of it.

Since the 1970s, second-generation trauma has appeared in cases where Holocaust-related trauma is transmitted from survivors to the subsequent generation.

I have two grown sons. My wife is American-born. My younger son was affected by my Holocaust experience but I don't know how I transmitted that trauma to him. I really don't know. I didn't share much with him about that. I only answered the questions he asked. No more. I didn't tell him stories. But he knew that I was a survivor. So he was affected mentally by my experiences, as he is to this day.

He once mentioned to me, 'You know, I was in the camp.' And I said, 'What?! You were not in the camp! I was!'

I wanted to bring him back to reality, so I said, 'You were not there! You were born here in the United States!' But that is an effect that the story of my past had on him. And who can tell about how the mind is affected by the horrors that he found out about, that I lived through. How did he absorb that? Did he learn about that from others? I don't know. But it's a sad part in my life.

For those who are traumatized, there can be so much pain that the person goes out of his/her body in order not to feel the pain. I did that in many ways. It's what helped me to survive. At the same time, there is much work to help people regain their true homes, their bodies. When they enter into their bodies, there's so much suffering. You can go through therapeutic work but it's not enough. The psychological approach is not enough. In the depths of their hearts, they do not know who they are. They are somehow lost. They have the feeling: 'I'm not right. If you would know the truth of me, you could not love me. And deep in me there is something wrong.' You have to   work on the level of the body. Traumatized people carry their memories in the cells of their bodies. Many trauma victims have had every diagnosis and they are not yet healed. But starting to work on the level of the cell, where the memories are carried, on a spiritual as well as psychological approach may help. The healing comes out of the depths. And in every person there is a place, which is holy. And if you can touch that place in the people, then you can bring up the source of healing.

In my journey of healing I have confronted negative experiences with the goal of hope. The journey may be said to be one of change and the *need* for change. Re-cognition, the reconstruction of positive realities interposed with what psychologists have termed 'restorative episodes', in counter-poise to negative ones, is the first step to dealing with and even overcoming trauma. Communication, or the sharing of experience, is something that initially led me to take the largest step in my healing: making my first film, completed in 1983. It was not easy. For the first time, I openly admitted the suffering I had experienced.

23 Why ...? A visit to Karlsruhe in Germany, 1997

After the war, I avoided returning to Germany. When I did go there, it was only as a transit stop on the way to Poland or other places in Europe. Until quite recently, it was a place where I would not consider having a holiday. Yet when it was connected with my work of healing and teaching, I would gladly go.

On my last stay in Germany several years ago, I was there with my friend, the Austrian violinist Herwig Strobl, whose father was a member of the Nazi party. Herwig was 5 years old at the end of the war so he couldn't do anything about what happened then. Now, Herwig plays improvised Yiddish music, many based on the Krakovian composer Mordechaj Gebirtig's songs.

On one break between going around playing, singing and talking about our experiences, I visited the city of Karlsruhe. Walking around, seeing the sites, I found myself in an old destroyed Catholic church. The ruins gave me the impression that it had been bombed, like so many places during the war. But I found out that it had been destroyed a long time before then – by the Protestants.

The ideology that has come out of our Western society seems to have been set against human beings and their right to believe different things – even between people of the same religion. When a fervent religious leader, army general or other political madman may set the fuse alight, society as a whole is responsible for what is done in its name. That's why I believe that politics will succeed only in a conscious humanity.

'Where's evil?' asks the Nazi propagandist in Kurt

Vonnegut's *Mother Night*. Answering himself he says, 'It's that large part of every man that wants to hate without limit, which wants to hate with God on his side. It's that part of every man that finds all kinds of ugliness so attractive. It's that part of an imbecile that punishes and vilifies and makes war gladly.'

To pitch even closer to why war takes place, along with its repeating undercurrent of lies, atrocities and denials, maybe we need to focus on the psychiatry behind it. We must raise the questions: Why do human beings quest revenge? What is it that makes some of us thirst for destruction? What is it in our subconscious that leads us to fight wars without any apparent shame? Where is our compassion?

A student of Gestalt Therapy founder Fritz Perls, Dr Harvey Wasserman, writes: 'Wars are caused by fear. Without fear, wars would be unnecessary. Culture stagnates and deteriorates because in the fear of change, they can't adapt ... Fear is a leftover, a childhood legacy that unfortunately persists into adulthood and corrupts and limits and tortures and deteriorates our lives'.

As a Jew born in Poland, I have been lucky enough to have had the possibility of telling you all these stories about what happened to me during the Holocaust. You don't have to agree with everything I have written, but I do hope that you will learn from what you have read. Out of the many stories I have heard, there's one healing statement that I would like to share, in the form of an old Woody Guthrie song I remember hearing from a rabbi named David Zeller. David said to me, 'Bernard, if you sing this song you will feel much better. Because if you've got troubles and you sing this song it makes your troubles go away. And if you have a question it will answer your question too'.

You can guess what I thought. 'Well, I already want to hear it!' I told David, 'What's the name of this song?'

'It's the "Why, oh why?" song', he said, 'It goes like this ...'

116

Here is what he sang:

> Why, oh why, oh why, oh why?
> Why, oh why, oh why?
> Because, because, because, because –
> Good bye, good bye, good bye ...

34. Bernard Offen (Bernard Offen)

Notes

1. Up to the end of 1939, eighty-seven priests and thirty-seven friars from the Kraków diocese were placed in concentration camps. Kurek (1997), pp. 43–4.
2. Poland had an estimated 3.3 million Jews out of 1939's recorded total population of 36 million. See Appendix.
3. Nelken (1999), pp. 122–5.
4. Zuckerman (1994), p.74, and Schindler (1997), p. 56.
5. Numbers 1–18 in this section are marked similarly on the Kraków Ghetto Map.
6. Bauminger (1986).
7. The museum is at Plac Bohaterów Getta 18. Open Mondays to Fridays between 10 am and 4 pm, and on Saturdays between 10 am and 2 pm. Closed on Sundays and national public holidays. Tel: (012) 6565625.
8. There were four hospitals in the ghetto: the Central Hospital; the Hospital for Chronic Diseases; the Hospital for Convalescent Care, a small hospital for elderly people on Limanowskiego Street; and the Hospital for Infectious Diseases that was transferred from Rękawka Street to Plac Zgody, following the division of the ghetto into two sections in 1943.
9. Halina Nelken records in her diary that one of the first round-ups occurred on 13 November 1941. Nelken (1999), p. 106.
10. Nelken (1999), p. 18.
11. Otto Wächter's statement of 1 December 1939 read: 'All Jews above 12 years of age should carry visible signs, namely a white band with the blue Star of David on the right arm of their outer garments. He is a Jew, who either is an adherent of the Judaic faith and everyone, whose fathers or mothers are or were of Judaic faith'.
12. Graf (1989), pp. 41–2.
13. Auxiliary police units utilized by the SS, comprising of ethnic Germans, and so-called Aryans from Latvia, Lithuania and the Ukraine. Poles with Aryan origins were also considered part of the *Volksdeutsche*.
14. See Ocholdo (1991).
15. There were three Julags: Julag I in Płaszów, Julag II in Prokocim, and Julag III in Bieżanów. The Julags were created following the agreement drawn between Hans Frank and Heinrich Himmler in June 1942 to implement Heydrich's 'Final Solution', decided at the Wannsee Conference earlier that year. In charge of the Julags was SS *Oberscharführer* Horst Pilarzik. SS *Oberscharführer* Müller was second in charge of Julag I, and also oversaw the building of the Płaszów camp.
16. Nelken (1999), p. 173.
17. 6,000 to 7,000 people were deported in June: 4,500 in October 1942.
18. Weinzierl (1997), pp. 134–9, 144–6 and 218–23. See also Madritsch (1962).
19. In spite of the so-called Tolerance Act declared in 1789 by Hapsburg Austrian Emperor Joseph II, prohibitions in selling liquors and leasing land, mills, and tolls

remained in force. Most of these were relaxed in 1868, a year after the election of the constitutional Austro-Hungarian Empire. Discriminatory marriage laws remained in force due to traditional national-religious legislation.

20. Nelken (1999), p. 164.
21. Graf (1989), p. 60.
22. Other deportees were sent to Majdanek. Prior to the liquidation of the ghetto, it is estimated that around 1,000 people were taken and killed at the Janowska camp near Lwów.
23. Although members of the SS were supposed to be only from the ranks of the Aryan *Übermenschen*, the situation of the war meant that some people were accepted into the SS if they showed they had Aryan blood.
24. Bieberstein (1985).
25. Many smaller ghettos existed through to 1943.
26. Nelken (1999), p. 189.
27. Graf (1989), p. 77. Some were transported to Bełżec or Sobibor. Nelken (1999), p. 190.

PART II: CHAPTERS 8–16

28. This map was made for the SS by Joseph Bau, a Jewish draftsman who had been employed to make signs for the Nazis since the ghetto period. Since Bau was useful to the Nazis, he was kept alive, and survived owing to his wife Rebecca, whom he met and married in Płaszów, adding his name to the list of workers who were to work at Oskar Schindler's factory in Czechoslovakia. See Bau (1998).
29. Chujowa Górka is said to have been used from the time that Jews from the Bochnia Ghetto arrived at Płaszów, 1–3 September 1943.
30. Duda (1992), p. 19.
31. Leah Goodman tells me that as a young child she was placed in a camp called Krakau-Kostrze on the outskirts of Kraków. This camp existed from the beginning of 1941 until March 1943, similar dates to the Kraków Ghetto's existence.
32. Another was Roman Spielman. Nelken (1999), p. 213.
33. Bau (1998), p. 152. The south-eastern part of Poland had once been western Ukraine, while the south-western part of Russia had been eastern Ukraine. Together they composed what had once been an independent nation-state. Referred to by Poles as Ukrainians, auxiliary German police formations made up of former citizens of the USSR sided with the Germans, hoping to have their independent status restored.
34. Graf writes about several *Wehrmacht* officers involved in procedures in the ghetto who, she claims, were contemptuous of both the SS and Gestapo. Graf (1989), pp. 62–7.
35. See Orenstein (1989), pp.188–208.
36. As a young girl, Anita Lobel, her brother and around half a dozen other Jews were kept secretly hidden by the Benedictine convent shelter in Kraków from 1941 until their being rounded-up during Christmas Day Mass in 1944. Lobel (1998), pp.54–80.
37. Prisoners included Jews from other ghettos, including Rzeszów, which had also been liquidated.
38. Before the war, Jakub Stendig was an engineer with the Kraków *kehilla* (Jewish community administration). After the murder of the engineer Diana Reiter, he was given the task of supervising the construction of the barracks. Stendig survived the war and wrote a book about Płaszów. Stendig (1946).
39. 35,000 according to Polish Supreme National Tribunal; 50,000 according to Meir Eldar (1999). See Appendix, Table 3.

40. A list of the survivors may be obtained from the Jewish Historical Institute: ul. Tłomackie 3/5, Warsaw 00-950.
41. Marber (2001), p. 93.
42. Bieberstein (1985), pp.100–38.
43. They had been betrayed by other Poles. Graf (1989), p. 118.
44. The Warsaw Ghetto was sealed on 25 November 1940; the Ghetto Uprising led by Marek Edelman took place on 19 April 1943. The separate Warsaw Uprising began on 1 August 1944, led by Polish leaders of the *Armia Krajowa* (Home Army).
45. Located on Montelupich Street, north of Stare Miasto and al. Słowackiego.
46. Graf (1989), p. 129.
47. Bau (1998). p. 140.
48. Ibid., p. 140. Inspectors from the International Red Cross also visited other camps.
49. Bieberstein (1985), pp. 134–5.
50. The transport meant to be sent to Oskar Schindler in Brünnlitz (*Sudetenland*) left Płaszów on 15 October 1944; the women were removed separately via Auschwitz. As Meir Eldar points out, since Goeth had been arrested the previous month, contrary to Steven Spielberg's film *Schindler's List* (based on Thomas Keneally's novel), he had no influence at the time the transport set out. Earlier, too, he had no influence, since the decision belonged solely to the concentration camp administration (*Amtsgruppe D*) in Berlin. This point, of course, does not exonerate Goeth's actions which, as noted, were especially callous. Goeth was personally guilty of ordering the murder of thousands of camp prisoners.
51. Many *kapos* and members of the *OD* who had inflicted suffering on prisoners were tried after the end of the war, convicted and hanged for collaborating with the Nazis. At the time of liberation, many were killed by barracks prisoners, or otherwise made to suffer for the tortures they had inflicted.
52. Graf (1989), p. 91.
53. Next to the *Appelplatz*, fire-ponds were constructed, several fires having occurred. The camp commandant ordered the new ponds to be filled with water. These proved to be a breeding ground for bugs and mosquitoes, in addition to the lice, fleas and bedbugs we had to endure.
54. Members of the Rosner family were musicians: Wiluś on trumpet, Herman on violin, Poldek on accordion. They made up the camp orchestra. Because Goeth enjoyed music, they were left to live and as a consequence survived the war. One brother died from pneumonia shortly after the end of the war. *Kapo* and *OD* man Haupenstock married one of the Rosners. Brecher (1994).
55. Bau (1998), p. 151.
56. Orenstein (1989), p. 182.
57. Graf (1989), p. 90 and Müller-Madej (1997), p. 218.
58. Nelken (1999), pp. 219, 238 and 246. Stella Müller-Madej mentions that *Bauleiter* Huth was kind to her uncle, after the two had met in Paris years before at an engineering conference. Müller-Madej (1997), pp. 110–12.
59. Statement made at Goeth's trial. Duda (1999).
60. Orenstein (1989), p.184.
61. The manager of the shoe factory was a young man called Mekhlovitz, named after his mother, a Polish Jewess, having been born out of wedlock. Although his German father was high in the Nazi Party, he was condemned to Płaszów because of his Jewish mother. Ferderber-Salz (1980), pp.124–26.
62. Graf (1989), p.124, and Bieberstein (1985) write that 286 children were included as part of a total of approximately 1,400 on the transport. Hungarian Jewish survivor Ana Novac's journal records her journey from Płaszów to Auschwitz and back to Płaszów between June and November 1944. In June she was sent from Auschwitz to Płaszów in a transport of 2,000 prisoners (Novac 1992, p. 55), and then returned to Auschwitz in July, this time in a transport of 10,000 Płaszów prisoners (Novac

1992, pp. 184–8). Novac survived following being placed in Section B, the Quarantine Camp.

63. Witness testimony of Mieczysław 'Mietek' Pemper, Goeth's personal secretary in the camp, at Goeth's trial.
64. Müller-Madej (1997), p. 275.
65. Nelken (1999), pp. 208–9 and Orenstein (1989), pp. 189–90. According to the latter, some of the Hungarian women arrived on 9 June 1944.
66. Offen (2005).
67. Orenstein (1989), pp. 197–8.
68. Graf (1989, p. 32.
69. On Joseph Bau's otherwise excellent map he misnames the two places of mass murder. This has been corrected in the copy included here.
70. Bau (1998), p. 152 and Graf (1989), p. 133.
71. 8,000 was the figure given by the Polish Supreme Court following the war, according to its interviews of first-hand witnesses. Wroński estimated that 150,000 people were processed through the camp. See Appendix, Table 3.
72. Similar to Chujowa Górka, the ditch Lipowy Dołek was known among prisoners as Cipowy Dołek (206).
73. Graf (1989), pp. 60–1; Schindler (1997), p. 64; Ferderber-Salz (1980), p. 132.
74. Graf (1989), p. 138.
75. According to Nelken (1999), pp. 238 and 241, this particular transport from Płaszów was to Częstochowa, Gross-Rosen and Auschwitz-Birkenau camps.

PART III: CHAPTERS 17–23

76. Near the Landsberg am Lech tower, where Hitler wrote *Mein Kampf* during his imprisonment after the failed *Putsch* in 1924.
77. Cichopek (2000).

Chronology

January 1941	expulsion of many Jews from Kraków. All Jews forced to clear snow from the street.

THE GHETTO PERIOD, 1941–43

3 March 1941	Order made forcing relocation of remaining Jews in Kraków to the Ghetto. Initial population: 15,000 to 17,000 people.
4 March 1941	Decree removes Jews and Romanies from official protection of the law.
15 March 1941	Order made declaring that Jews allowed to use public transport only with a special permit from the *Stadthauptmann* (city commandant).
21 March 1941	Closure of the ghetto.
May 1941	Jews from twenty-one villages surrounding Kraków ordered to move to the ghetto. *My older brothers Sam and Nathan disappear from the ghetto.*
15 October 1941	Jews not allowed to leave the ghetto, under threat of death.
27–29 December 1941	Jews ordered to hand over all furs.
20 January 1942	Wannsee Conference: Nazi meeting planning the 'Final Solution'. Mass killing begins.
1 June 1942	The ghetto is sealed and the first major deportation from the Kraków Ghetto of 5,000 residents to Bełżec extermination camp takes place.
4 June 1942	Bloody Thursday massacre in ghetto square.
8 June 1942	Second deportation from ghetto. Reduction of ghetto. *My family moved from Krakusa Street 9 to Limanowskiego Street 5.*
Summer 1942	Construction of the Płaszów camp begins.
27–28 October 1942	Deportation of 6,000 Jews to Bełżec or Majdanek. 600 shot in ghetto. *My mother, Rochme Gitel Schifer, and my sister Miriam are deported.* *They disappear from my life while I am on a food-smuggling trip outside the Kraków Ghetto.*
November 1942	Ghetto divided into sections A and B. Workers separated from old, young and sick.
24 December 1942	Jewish resistance (*ŻOB*) fighters attack SS men at Restauracja Cyganeria.
13 March 1943	Liquidation of Kraków Ghetto A. Relocation to Płaszów forced labor camp. 700 shot in ghetto. *My father, brothers and I are marched to Płaszów concentration camp.*
14 March 1943	Liquidation of the Kraków Ghetto B. Mass killing and transport of prisoners to Auschwitz-Birkenau.

PŁASZÓW CONCENTRATION CAMP, 1942–45

28 October 1942	Decision made to construct a camp at Płaszów.
11 February 1943	SS-*Sturmbannführer* Amon Leopold Goeth takes over leadership of the camp. Płaszów becomes a labor camp with branches in Mielec and Wieliczka.
17/18 March 1943?	*I escape from Płaszów.*
March 1943	*I am 'smuggled' into Julag I.*
March–April 1943	Himmler and Hitler draft the *Informe Korherr* which confirms, on the basis of statistical data received from the SS, that by the end of 1942 the Nazis have been responsible for the deaths of 4 million European Jews.
August 1943	Liquidation of Julag I. *I am transferred back to the Płaszów labor camp.*
September 1943	Tarnów Ghetto liquidated; inhabitants sent to the Płaszów camp.
November 1943	Julag II and III liquidated. All 1,500 women are sent to the Płaszów camp to work in the Hasag munitions factory in Skarzysko-Kamienna. Male prisoners are sent to a similar factory in Częstochowa.
10 January 1944	Płaszów becomes a concentration camp.
7 May 1944	'Health Review' at Płaszów. One week later a transfer to Auschwitz takes place of 1,500 children, elderly and infirm people – those considered useless for work purposes.
14 May 1944	Transport of children from the *Kinderheim.*
August 1944	*My father, two brothers Sam and Nathan and I are sent to Mauthausen.*
6 August 1944	Black Sunday – over 7,000 people arrested in Kraków.
24 August 1944	*Arrival at Auschwitz-Birkenau. Following selection, I am separated from my father for the final time.*
27 August 1944	Liquidation of Płaszów camp begins. Barracks disassembled.
23 September 1944	Amon Goeth is arrested for corruption and embezzlement.
27 October 1944	*I am transferred from Auschwitz-Birkenau to Dachau-Kaufering.*
14 January 1945	Final transports from Płaszów to Auschwitz. Around 8,000 people remaining in Płaszów camp are killed.
18 January. 1945	Kraków liberated.
26 January 1945	Auschwitz is liberated by Soviet troops.
2 May 1945	*Following a Death March from Kaufering (near Landsberg) to near Wolfrats-Hausen, I am liberated by the US Army.*

Appendix:
Population of Kraków and number of prisoners in the ghetto and Płaszów camp

TABLE 1
JEWISH POPULATION IN KRAKÓW, 1900–55

Poland had an estimated 3.3 million Jews out of the 1931 census-recorded total population of 36 million: almost 10 per cent of the country's total population. Registered Jewish population of Kraków (as percentage of total population) was as follows: 1900: 25,670 (28 per cent); 1921: 45,229 (28 per cent); 1938: approx. 60,000 (25 per cent). In 1948, after the war, the registered Jewish population was 5,900 (2 per cent). In 2000, the Jewish population of Kraków was estimated at fewer than 200.

Year	Jewish Population	Total Population	per cent
1900	25,670	91,310	28
1910	32,321	143,000	23
1921	45,229	164,000	28
1931	56,800	219,286	26
1938	60,000	237,532	25
1939	68,482		
1948	5,900	299,565	2
1955	*4,000	335,000	1
2000	>200	750,000	0.2

* approximation

Source: Encyclopedia Judaica.

TABLE 2
PRISONERS OF PŁASZÓW CAMP, 1942–44

Although it is the intention that the figures appearing in this book are as accurate as possible, there are difficulties with assessing the exact number of people at any given time in either the Kraków Ghetto or Płaszów camp, owing to the constant fluctuation of the population.

According to the Polish Supreme Court, 8,000 people were killed in the camp, out of the estimated total of 35,000 (Polish Supreme Court) and 50,000 prisoners (Meir Eldar, 1999) who are estimated to have passed through the camp; 150,000 according to Wroński (1981a).

Prisoners included around 20,000 Jews from Poland and Hungary, approximately 4,000 Polish non-Jews and several dozen Romany families.

Out of a population of around 3.3 million Jews in pre-war Poland, an estimated 3 million Polish Jews perished in the Second World War. It is considered that between 120,000 and 200,000 (Directorate of Polish Civil Resistance) Polish Jews survived the Holocaust, mostly by hiding under false non-Jewish papers or in exile.

Date	Recorded transfers of Płaszów camp prisoner population (approximate figures)
Summer 1942	Construction of Płaszów labor camp begins.
Fall 1942	Polish Jews comprise initial camp population of 2,000.
11 February 1943	Amon Goeth transferred to Kraków.
13 March 1943	6,000 increase to camp population due to liquidation of Kraków Ghetto. Polish non-Jews and several dozen Roma families sent to camp.
August 1943	Jewish prisoner population increases following closure of Julags I-III.
September 1943	2,000 Jews from Tarnów Ghetto sent to Płaszów camp.
21 February 1944	260 male prisoners sent to *KL* Auschwitz.[a]
April 1944	Transport of prisoners from Majdanek.[b]
May 1944	1,300 Hungarian Jews arrive at Płaszów, mostly women[c] sent to Auschwitz and gassed.[d]
7 May 1944	Following 'Health Review', 1,500 sick transported to Auschwitz-Birkenau.
14 May 1944	Transport of children from the *Kinderheim*.
15 May 1944	Transport of Hungarian Jews to Auschwitz;[e] they were told that they would be exchanged for German POWs.
May–June 1944	Population of camp reaches high point of approximately

	22,000–24,000. Liquidation of Płaszów. Prisoners sent to Mauthausen, Brünnlitz, Częstochowa, Gross-Rosen, Stutthof, Flossenbürg or Auschwitz-Birkenau.
August 1944	6,000 to 8,000 Hungarian Jews sent to Płaszów camp.
2 August 1944	1,414 female prisoners, some from Hungary, sent to *KL* Auschwitz.[a]
10 August 1944	10,000 prisoners of Płaszów sent to Auschwitz and Mauthausen; 10 per cent of workers from the Madritsch factory.[f]
11 August 1944	1,999 female prisoners, Hungarian and Polish, sent to *KL* Auschwitz.[a]
27 August 1944	Liquidation of Płaszów camp begins. Barracks disassembled.[f]
13 September 1944	Goeth arrested on corruption charges. Replaced by Arnold Buscher.
5 October 1944	Approximately 200 men sent to Gross-Rosen and 300 women to *KL* Auschwitz.[f]
15 October 1944	Transfer from Płaszów of Polish prisoners to work near Tarnów and the concentration camp at Gross-Rosen.[c] 1,000 Jews to Brünnlitz (Schindler factory).
21–22 October 1944	Transfer of 2,000 Płaszów female prisoners to *KL* Auschwitz-Birkenau.[a] Around 600 prisoners including 40 German *Kapos* and a few Poles remain. 300 Jewish women sent to Schindler's Brünnlitz factory.[c]
January 1945	Final transports to Auschwitz.
15 January 1945	Płaszów concentration camp liquidated, three days before the Soviet liberation of Kraków.

Sources:

(a)	Czech (1990).
(b)	Orenstein (1989).
(c)	Graf (1989), p. 127.
(d)	Nelken (1999), p. 229.
(e)	Korboski (1989), p. 53.
(f)	Wienzierl (1997), p. 138

Bibliography

Akavia, Miriam. 1995. *An End to Childhood*, Library of Holocaust Testimonies. London: Vallentine Mitchell.

Aaron, Frieda W. (ed.) 1990. *Bearing the Unbearable: Yiddish and Polish Poetry in the Ghettos and Concentration Camps* (includes poetry by Joseph Bau written in Płaszów). Albany, NY: SUNY Press.

Bau, Joseph. 1998. *Dear God, Have You Ever Gone Hungry?* New York: Arcade Publishing.

Bauminger, Arieh L. 1986. *The Fighters of the Cracow Ghetto*. Jerusalem: Keter Press.

Bieberstein, Aleksander. 1985. *Zagłada Żydów w Krakowie*. Kraków: Wydawnictwo Literackie.

Bogner, Nahum. 2000. *The Convent Children: The Rescue of Jewish Children in Polish Convents During the Holocaust*. Jerusalem: Yad Vashem Studies XXVII, 2.

Brecher, Elinor J. 1994. *Schindler's Legacy: True Stories of the List Survivors*. New York: Plume/Penguin.

Breitman, Richard. 1998. *Official Secrets: What the Nazis Planned, What the British and Americans Knew*. New York: Hall & Wang.

Cichopek, Anna. 2000. *Pogrom Żydów w Krakowie 11 Sierpnia 1945 R.* Warszawa: Żydowski Instytut Historyczny.

Czajkowski, Jacek. 1997. *Kardynał Adam Stefan Sapieha*. Wrocław: Ossolineum.

Czech, Danuta. 1990. *Auschwitz Chronicle*. New York: Henry Holt.

Datner, Szymon. 1968. *Las sprawiedliwych: karta z dziejów ratownictwa Żydów w okupowanej Polsce* [*The Forest of the Just: A Page from History of Rescuing Jews in Occupied Poland*]. Warszawa: Książka i Wiedza.

Davies, Norman. 1981. *God's Playground*, vol. II. New York: Oxford University Press.

————. 1986. *Heart of Europe: A Short History of Poland.* New York: Oxford University Press.

Davies, Norman, and Moorhouse, Roger. 2002. *Microcosm: Portrait of a Central European City.* London: Jonathan Cape.

Dokumenty zbrodni i męczeństwa. 1946. Kraków: Wojewódzka Żydowska Komisja.

Draenger, Gusta. 1996. *Justyna's Narrative.* Amherst, MA: University of Massachusetts Press.

Duda, Eugeniusz. 1991. *Krakowskie judaica.* Warszawa: Wydawnictwo PTTK 'KRAJ'.

————. 1999. *The Jews of Cracow.* Kraków: Wydawnictwo 'Hagada'.

Ferderber-Salz, Bertha. 1968. *And the Sun Kept Shining.* New York: Holocaust Library.

Graf, Malvina. 1989. *The Kraków Ghetto and the Płaszów Camp Remembered.* Tallahassee, FL: Florida State University Press.

Gross, Jan Tomasz. 2001. *Neighbors.* Princeton, NJ: Princeton University Press.

Gross, Nathan et al. 1986? *Pozostała tylko legenda...* [*Only The Legend Remains/Vy'notra rak agada...*]. Tel Aviv: Ekked Publishing House (this book comprises 10 items, several written in Polish, by eleven authors: Arthur Fischer, Meir Bosak, Nathan Gross, Miriam Akavia, Halina Nelken, Felicia Schechter-Karay, Irene Rothberg-Bronner, Joseph Bau, Jospeh Bosak, Miriam and Mordecai Peleg).

Gutman, Yisrael. 1986. 'Polish and Jewish Historiography on the Question of Polish–Jewish Relations During World War II'. In *The Jews in Poland.* Kraków: Fundacja Judaica, Jagiellonian University Press.

Halkowski, Henryk. 1998. *The Legends from the Jewish Town in Kazimierz near Cracow.* Kraków: Mercury.

Hilberg, Raul. 1985. *The Destruction of the European Jews.* New York: Holmes & Meir.

Hoffman, Ewa. 1998. *Shtetl: The Life and Death of a Small Town and the World of Polish Jews.* London: Secker & Warburg.

Holocaust Survivor Testimonies Catalogue Vol.I. Warsaw: Jewish Historical Institute Archives, Record Group 301/Nos.1–900, 1998.

Holocaust Survivor Testimonies Catalogue Vol.II. Warsaw: Jewish Historical Institute Archives, Record Group 301/Nos.901–2000, 2000.

Hundert, Gershon D. 1992. 'Jews and Other Poles'. In *The Jews in a Polish Private Town*. London: John Hopkins University Press (pp.36–45).

Jacobs, Norman. 2002. 'Film as Dialogue and the Process of Healing'. In *Children and the Holocaust*. Kraków: Jagiellonian University Press (pp.59–68).

Kapralski, Sławomir (ed.) 1999. *The Jews in Poland (Vol.II)*. Kraków: Fundacja Judaica, Jageillonian University Press.

Karpf, Anne. 1997. *The War After: Living with the Holocaust*. London: Minerva,.

Kiełkowski, Roman. 1981. *Zlikwidować na miejscu! Z dziejów okupacji hitlerowskiej w Krakowie*. Kraków: Wydawnictwo Literackie.

Korboński, Stefan. 1989. *The Jews and Poles in World War II*. New York: Hippocrene Books.

Kunicka-Wyrzykowska, Magdalena. 1982. *Biuletyn Głównej Komisji Badania Zbrodni przeciwko Narodowi Polskiemu*, vol. 31. Warszawa.

Kurek, Ewa. 1997. *Your Life Is Worth Mine*. New York: Hippocrene Books.

Lendvai, Paul. 1971. *Anti-Semitism in Eastern Europe*. London: Macdonald.

Ligocka, Roma. 2002. *The Girl in the Red Coat*. London: Sceptre Books.

Lobel, Anita. 1998. *No Pretty Pictures*. New York: Avon Camelot.

Lukas, Richard C. 1986. *Out of the Inferno: Poles Remember the Holocaust*. Kentucky: University Press of Kentucky.

———. 1997. *The Forgotten Holocaust: The Poles Under German Occupation 1939–44*. New York: Hippocrene Books.

Lukowski, Jerzy, and Zawadzki, Hubert. 2001. *A Concise History of Poland*. Cambridge: Cambridge University Press.

Madritsch, Julius. 1962. *Menschen In Not! Meine Erlebnisse in den Jahren 1940 bis 1944 als Unternehmer im damaligen Generalgouvernement*. Wien: Selbstverlag.

Mayer, Arno J. 1988. *Why Did the Heavens Not Darken? The Final Solution in History.* New York: Pantheon.

Miłosz, Czesław. 2000. *The 1999 Aleksander and Alicja Hertz Annual Memorial Lecture,* trans. M. Jacobs. Kraków: Judaica Foundation Centre for Jewish Culture.

Melezin, Abraham. 1946. *Przyczynek do znajomości stosunków demograficznych wsród ludności Żydowskiej w Łodzi, Krakowie i Lublinie podczas okupacji niemieckiej.* Łodź.

Müller-Madej, Stella. 1997. *A Girl from Schindler's List.* London: Polish Cultural Foundation.

Nelken, Halina. 1999. *And Yet, I Am Here!* Amherst, MA: University of Massachusetts Press.

Novac, Ana. 1997. *The Beautiful Days of My Youth: Six Months in Auschwitz and Płaszów.* New York: Henry Holt.

Offen, Sam. 2005. *When Hope Prevails.* Livonia, MI: First Page Publications.

Olchodo, André. 1991. *Chansons Yiddish.* Gdańsk: 'Graf'.

Oppenheim, Bogdan W. (ed.) 2001. *The Polish Catholic Church and the Struggle Against Anti-Semitism.* Kraków: Judaica Foundation.

Orenstein, Henry. 1989. *I SHALL LIVE: Surviving Against All Odds 1939–1945.* New York: Touchstone Books.

Paluch, Andrzej K. (ed.) 1992. *The Jews in Poland (Vol.I).* Kraków: Fundacja Judaica, Jageillonian University Press.

Pankiewicz, Tadeusz. 1985. *The Cracow Ghetto Pharmacy,* second edn. New York: Holocaust Library.

Pióro, Anna, and Karliska, Wiesława. 1995. *Kraków Getto.* Kraków: Dom Kultury 'Podgórze'.

Pogonowski, Iwo Cyprian. 1988. *Jews in Poland: A Documentary History.* New York: Hippocrene Books.

Polonsky, Antony (ed.) 1990. *'My Brother's Keeper?' Recent Polish Debates on the Holocaust.* London: Routledge.

Proces Ludobójcy Amona Leopolda Goetha przed Najwyższym Trybunałem Narodowym. 1947. Warszawa, Łódź, Kraków: Jewish Historical Institute.

Ringelblum, Emmanuel. 1992. *Polish–Jewish Relations during the Second World War.* Illinois: Northwestern University Press.

Rufeisen-Schupper, Hela. 1996. *Pożegnanie Miłej 18*. Kraków: Wydawnictwo 'Beseder'.

Scharf, Rafael F. 1999. *Poland, What Have I To Do With Thee...: Essays Without Prejudice*. Kraków: Fundacja Judaica.

Schindler, Emilie. 1997. *Where Light and Shadow Meet*. New York: W.W. Norton.

Staner, Mieczysław. 1999. *The Eyewitness*. Kraków: Wydawnictwo 'Hagada' and Arjona-Jarden.

Staner, Mike. 1999. *Ties of Blood*. Kraków: Sofer.

Stendig, Jakub. 1946. *Płaszów (obóz)*. Kraków: Wojewódzka Żydowska Komisja Historyczna (published in Hebrew, *Płaszów: The Last Stop for the Jews of Kraków*. 1970. Tel Aviv: Menorah, courtesy Jewish Historical Institute, Warsaw).

Stern, Fritz. 2001. *Einstein's German World*. London: Penguin Books.

Taubenschlag, Stanisław. 1998. *To Be a Jew in Occupied Poland*. Oświęcim: 'Frap-Books'.

Tec, Nechama. 1985. *When Light Pierced the Darkness: Christian Rescue of Jews in Nazi-Occupied Poland*. New York: Oxford University Press.

Tencer, Gołda. 1998. *I Still See Their Eyes*. Warsaw: Fundacja Shalom.

Torańska, Teresa. 1987. *'Them': Stalin's Polish Puppets*. New York: Perennial Library.

Under One Heaven. 1998. Warsaw: WI special issue.

W 3-cią Rocznicę Zagłady Getta w Krakowie (13.III.1943–13.III.1946). 1946. Wojewódzka Żydowska Komisja Historyczna.

Weinzierl, Erika. 1997. *Zu Wenig Gerechte: Österreicher und Judenverfolgung 1938–1945*. Graz/Wien/Köln: Styria.

Wroński, Tadeusz. 1974. *Kronika okupowanego Krakowa*. Kraków: Wydawnictwo Literackie.

———. 1981a. *Obóz w Płaszowie: 1942–45*. Warszawa: Wydawnictwo 'Sport i Turystyka'.

———. 1981b. *'Liban': Karny obóz Służby Budowlanej w Krakowie w latach 1942–44*. Warszawa: Wydawnictwo 'Sport I Turystyka'.

Zar, Rose. 1992. *In the Mouth of the Wolf*. Philadelphia: Jewish Publication Society.

Zuckerman, Abraham. 1994. *A Voice in the Chorus*. Stamford: Longmeadow Press.

Films

Faniszyn, Wiktor. Underground film of Płaszów Camp: winter 1944–45 (available via Muzeum Historyczne Miasta Krakowa).

Film recording the destruction of Burial Society Building in Płaszów Camp (available via Muzeum Historyczne Miasto Krakowa).Offen, Bernard. 1983. *The Work*.

Offen, Bernard. 1997. *My Hometown Concentration Camp*.

Offen, Bernard. 1999. *Process B-7815*.

Offen, Bernard. 2003. *Hawaii and the Holocaust*.

Offen, Bernard, 2007. *Return to Auschwitz* (all productions are available via www.bernardoffen.org).

Website

Bernard Offen, www.bernardoffen.org

Useful addresses

Jewish Historical Institute
ul. Tłomackie 3/5
Warszawa 00-950
Tel: (022) 827-1843

Polish National Memory Institute
Plac Krasińskich 2/4/6
Warszawa
Tel: (022) 530-90-89 Fax: (022) 530-90-89

Muzeum Historyczne Miasta Krakowa
Rynek Główny 35
Kraków